FINANCIAL INSTITUTIONS AND SERVICES

THE COMMUNITY DEVELOPMENT FINANCIAL INSTITUTIONS FUND

FINANCIAL INSTITUTIONS AND SERVICES

Additional books in this series can be found on Nova's website under the Series tab.

Additional E-books in this series can be found on Nova's website under the E-book tab.

FINANCIAL INSTITUTIONS AND SERVICES

THE COMMUNITY DEVELOPMENT FINANCIAL INSTITUTIONS FUND

ANDRE L. WRIGHT
EDITOR

NOVINKA

New York

For permission to use material from this book please contact us:
Telephone 631-231-7269; Fax 631-231-8175
Web Site: http://www.novapublishers.com

Library of Congress Cataloging-in-Publication Data

ISBN: 978-1-62417-551-0

Published by Nova Science Publishers, Inc. †New York

CONTENTS

Preface		**vii**
Chapter 1	Community Development Financial Institutions (CDFI) Fund: Programs and Policy Issues *Sean Lowry*	**1**
Chapter 2	New Markets Tax Credit: An Introduction *Donald J. Marples*	**41**
Chapter 3	Community Development Financial Institutions and New Markets Tax Credit Programs in Metropolitan and Nonmetropolitan Areas *United States Government Accountability Office*	**53**
Chapter 4	Testimony of Donna J. Gambrell, Director, CDFI Fund. Hearing on "Community Development Financial Institutions (CDFIs): Their Unique Role and Challenges Serving Lower-Income, Underserved and Minority Communities"	**87**
Index		**99**

PREFACE

As communities face a variety of economic challenges, some are looking to local banks and financial institutions for solutions that address the specific development needs of low-income and distressed communities. Community development financial institutions (CDFIs) provide financial products and services, such as mortgage financing for homebuyers and not-for-profit developers, underwriting and risk capital for community facilities; technical assistance; and commercial loans and investments to small, start-up, or expanding businesses. CDFIs include regulated institutions, such as community development banks and credit unions, and non-regulated institutions, such as loan and venture capital funds. This book describes the Fund's history, current appropriations, and each of its programs. A description of the Fund's process of certifying certain financial institutions to be eligible for the Fund's program award is discussed, as is the program's purpose, use of award proceeds, eligibility criteria, and relevant issues for Congress.

Chapter 1 – As communities face a variety of economic challenges, some are looking to local banks and financial institutions for solutions that address the specific development needs of low-income and distressed communities. Community development financial institutions (CDFIs) provide financial products and services, such as mortgage financing for homebuyers and not-for-profit developers, underwriting and risk capital for community facilities; technical assistance; and commercial loans and investments to small, start-up, or expanding businesses. CDFIs include regulated institutions, such as community development banks and credit unions, and non-regulated institutions, such as loan and venture capital funds. The Community Development Financial Institutions Fund (the Fund), an agency within the

Department of the Treasury, administers several programs that encourage the role of CDFIs, and similar organizations, in community development.

Nearly 1,000 financial institutions located throughout all 50 states are eligible for the Fund's programs to provide financial and technical assistance to meet the needs of businesses, homebuyers, community developers, and investors in distressed communities. In addition, the Fund allocates the New Markets Tax Credit to more than 5,000 eligible investment vehicles in low-income communities (LICs). This report begins by describing the Fund's history, current appropriations, and each of its programs. A description of the Fund's process of certifying certain financial institutions to be eligible for the Fund's program awards follows. The next section provides an overview of each program's purpose, use of award proceeds, eligibility criteria, and relevant issues for Congress. The final section analyzes four policy considerations of congressional interest, regarding the Fund and the effective use of federal resources to promote economic development. First, it analyzes the debate on targeting development assistance toward particular geographic areas or low-income individuals generally. Prior research indicates that geographically targeted assistance, like the Fund's programs, may increase economic activity in the targeted place or area. However, this increase may be due to a shift in activity from an area not eligible for assistance. Second, it analyzes the debate over targeting economic development policies toward labor or capital. The Fund's programs primarily rely on the latter, such as encouraging lending to small businesses, rather than targeting labor, such as wage subsidies. Research indicates the benefits of policies that reduce capital costs in a targeted place may not be passed on to local laborers, in the form of higher wages or increased employment. Third, it examines whether the Fund plays a unique role in promoting economic development, or if it duplicates, compliments, or competes with the goals and activities of other federal, state, and local programs. Although CDFIs are eligible for other federal assistance programs and other agencies have a similar mission as the Fund, the Fund's programs have a particular emphasis on encouraging private investment and building the capacity of private financial entities to enhance local economic development Fourth, it examines assessments of the Fund's management. Some argue that the Fund's programs are not managed in an effective manner and are not held to appropriate performance measures. Others argue that the Fund is fulfilling its mission and achieving its performance measures.

Chapter 2 – The New Markets Tax Credit (NMTC) is a non-refundable tax credit intended to encourage private capital investment in eligible, impoverished, low-income communities. NMTCs are allocated by the

Community Development Financial Institutions Fund (CDFI), a bureau within the United States Department of the Treasury, under a competitive application process. Investors who make qualified equity investments reduce their federal income tax liability by claiming the credit. The NMTC program, enacted in 2000, is currently authorized to allocate \$33 billion through the end of 2011. To date, the CDFI has exhausted through 664 awards totaling \$33 billion in NMTC's allocation authority. The 111th Congress extended and modified the NMTC program authorization. The American Recovery and Reinvestment Tax Act of 2009, P.L. 111-5, increased the NMTC allocation for 2008 and 2009 to \$5 billion from \$3.5 billion. Further, the Tax Relief, Unemployment Insurance Reauthorization, and Job Creation Act of 2010 (P.L. 111-312) extended the NMTC authorization through 2011 at \$3.5 billion per year. In the 112th Congress H.R. 2655 and H.R. 3224 would both extend the NMTC through 2016 with allocation authority of \$5 billion \$10 billion, respectively.

Chapter 3 – Report by United States Government Accountability Office, GAO-12-547R, dated April 26, 2012.

Chapter 4 – Testimony of Donna J. Gambrell, Director, CDFI Fund.

In: The Community Development ...
Editor: Andre L. Wright
ISBN: 978-1-62417-551-0

Chapter 1

COMMUNITY DEVELOPMENT FINANCIAL INSTITUTIONS (CDFI) FUND: PROGRAMS AND POLICY ISSUES*

Sean Lowry

SUMMARY

As communities face a variety of economic challenges, some are looking to local banks and financial institutions for solutions that address the specific development needs of low-income and distressed communities. Community development financial institutions (CDFIs) provide financial products and services, such as mortgage financing for homebuyers and not-for-profit developers, underwriting and risk capital for community facilities; technical assistance; and commercial loans and investments to small, start-up, or expanding businesses.

CDFIs include regulated institutions, such as community development banks and credit unions, and non-regulated institutions, such as loan and venture capital funds.

The Community Development Financial Institutions Fund (the Fund), an agency within the Department of the Treasury, administers several programs that encourage the role of CDFIs, and similar organizations, in community

* This is an edited, reformatted and augmented version of the Congressional Research Service Publication, CRS Report for Congress R42770, dated October 3, 2012.

development. Nearly 1,000 financial institutions located throughout all 50 states are eligible for the Fund's programs to provide financial and technical assistance to meet the needs of businesses, homebuyers, community developers, and investors in distressed communities. In addition, the Fund allocates the New Markets Tax Credit to more than 5,000 eligible investment vehicles in low-income communities (LICs).

This report begins by describing the Fund's history, current appropriations, and each of its programs. A description of the Fund's process of certifying certain financial institutions to be eligible for the Fund's program awards follows. The next section provides an overview of each program's purpose, use of award proceeds, eligibility criteria, and relevant issues for Congress.

The final section analyzes four policy considerations of congressional interest, regarding the Fund and the effective use of federal resources to promote economic development. First, it analyzes the debate on targeting development assistance toward particular geographic areas or low-income individuals generally. Prior research indicates that geographically targeted assistance, like the Fund's programs, may increase economic activity in the targeted place or area. However, this increase may be due to a shift in activity from an area not eligible for assistance.

Second, it analyzes the debate over targeting economic development policies toward labor or capital. The Fund's programs primarily rely on the latter, such as encouraging lending to small businesses, rather than targeting labor, such as wage subsidies.

Research indicates the benefits of policies that reduce capital costs in a targeted place may not be passed on to local laborers, in the form of higher wages or increased employment.

Third, it examines whether the Fund plays a unique role in promoting economic development, or if it duplicates, compliments, or competes with the goals and activities of other federal, state, and local programs. Although CDFIs are eligible for other federal assistance programs and other agencies have a similar mission as the Fund, the Fund's programs have a particular emphasis on encouraging private investment and building the capacity of private financial entities to enhance local economic development

Fourth, it examines assessments of the Fund's management. Some argue that the Fund's programs are not managed in an effective manner and are not held to appropriate performance measures. Others argue that the Fund is fulfilling its mission and achieving its performance measures.

INTRODUCTION

Community development financial institutions (CDFIs) have been using small-scale, and locally developed strategies to stabilize and advance low-income and financially underserved communities for decades. CDFIs are specialized financial institutions that work in market niches that are underserved by traditional financial institutions. They provide a range of financial products and services in economically distressed markets, such as mortgage financing for low-income and first-time homebuyers and not-for-profit developers, flexible underwriting and risk capital for needed community facilities, technical assistance, and commercial loans and investments to small start-up or expanding businesses in low-income areas. CDFIs exist in both rural and urban communities. CDFIs include regulated institutions, such as community development banks and credit unions, and non-regulated institutions, such as loan and venture capital funds.

TYPES OF CDFIS

- *Depository institutions* offer a range of consumer and institutional savings, checking, and lending services. This group includes for-profit community development banks and non-profit community development credit unions. These CDFIS are regulated and insured by the same agencies that govern other banks and credit unions.
- *Loan funds* are non-regulated, non-profit institutions that focus on one or more aspects of capital access and community development, such as small business lending, home mortgage financing, and community facilities development financing.
- *Community development venture capital funds* are for-profit or non-profit institutions that deliver equity capital to businesses in distressed communities.
- *Community development intermediaries* facilitate various revitalization activities between large investors and a defined population of community development corporations, CDFIs, or non-profit organizations.

Source: Federal Reserve Bank of Richmond, "Community Development Financial Institutions: A Unique Partnership for Banks," *Community Development Special Issue*, 2011.

Community banks also play a role in economic recovery. The success of these banks is often linked with local communities; businesses and individuals need the financial services that community banks provide, while the banks need opportunities for profitable lending.[1] Some are specifically concerned that a shortage of credit from community banks will reduce the abilities for new entrepreneurs to establish a business, existing businesses to expand and hire new workers, and for consumers to acquire the credit they need to buy or make improvements to a property.

This report begins by describing the Community Development Financial Institutions Fund's (Fund's) history, current appropriations, and each of its programs. The next section of the report analyzes four policy considerations of congressional interest, regarding the Fund and the effective use of federal resources to promote economic development. It analyzes the reasons why some individuals may choose not to locate in an underdeveloped community, why government policies may be justified to encourage economic activity to relocate to underdeveloped communities, and which policies are more successful in addressing aspects of underdevelopment. Lastly, this report examines the Fund's programs and management to see if they represent an effective and efficient government effort to promote economic development in low-income and distressed communities.

The Riegle Community Development and Regulatory Improvement Act of 1994 (P.L. 103-325) established the Community Development Financial Institutions Fund to assist CDFIs in providing coordinated development strategies across various sectors of the local economy. These coordinated development strategies are designed to encourage small businesses, affordable housing, the availability of commercial real estate, and human development.[2] The legislation intended to improve the supply of capital, credit, private investment, and development services in economically distressed areas. In proposing the Fund, President Clinton stated that, "by ensuring greater access to capital and credit, we will tap the entrepreneurial energy of America's poorest communities and enable individuals and communities to become self-sufficient."[3]

Though the Riegle Act created the Fund as a wholly owned, independent government corporation, a supplemental appropriations bill moved the Fund into the Department of Treasury (Treasury) in 1995.[4] The Fund was moved within Treasury because of its focus on financial institutions and because other bank regulatory agencies (i.e., the Office of Thrift Supervision and Office of the Comptroller of the Currency) were already located within the agency.[5] The Fund is a component of the programs of the Under Secretary's Office of

Domestic Finance, and it is directly under the Assistant Secretary for Financial Institutions.[6]

The Fund is headed by a director, who is appointed by the Secretary of the Treasury and not subject to Senate confirmation. Initially, the director served a three-year term, however the Fund was led by approximately 10 directors in its first 15 years. To bring greater stability to the Fund's leadership, the Secretary of the Treasury made the director's position into a career appointment in 2010, meaning that there are no limits on the length of the director's term.[7]

By statute, the Fund also has a 15-member Community Development Advisory Board. The board members include the Secretaries of Agriculture, Commerce, Housing and Urban Development (HUD), Interior, Treasury, the Administrator of the Small Business Administration (SBA), and nine private citizens appointed by the President. The Advisory Board's function is to advise the director of the Fund on the policies regarding the Fund's activities. The Advisory Board is not allowed, by law, to advise the Fund on the granting or denial of any particular application for monetary or non-monetary awards.

Although the Fund is organized within Treasury's Office of Domestic Finance, in recent years Congress has provided the Fund with its own budget authority line in annual financial services appropriations bills.[8] These appropriations go toward the administration of the Fund, its programs, and program awards. The Fund's appropriations cover administration of approvals for allocations of the New Markets Tax Credit (NMTC); however, the actual tax credit is awarded through the Internal Revenue Code, not through the Fund's appropriations.

As shown in **Table 1**, the Fund's enacted budget authority for FY2012 is $221 million. Of this $221 million, 66.1% (approximately $146 million) appropriated for the Fund's core CDFI assistance programs; 10.4% (approximately $23 million) appropriated for administration of the Fund's programs, including the NMTC; and the remaining 23.5% ($52 million) appropriated for set-asides for other, specific programs. For FY2012, the Fund has awarded approximately $187 million to 210 organizations in 41 states.[9]

As shown in **Table 1**, the Obama Administration's budget request for FY2013 is the same amount ($221 million) enacted for the Fund for FY2012. However, the Administration has requested somewhat higher levels of funding for the Healthy Food Financing Initiative, as well as an initial appropriation of $20.0 million for the Bank on USA program.[10] The Administration has requested that the additional funding for these programs come from the share of funding previously allocated to the CDFI program and Fund's administration.

Table 1. Community Development Financial Institutions (CDFI) Fund Programs Funding, FY2012 Enacted and FY2013 Request (in millions of dollars)

Budget Activity	FY2012 Enacted	FY2013 Request
CDFI Program	$146,035	$127,953
Administration	22,965	21,047
Healthy Food Financing Initiative	22	25
Bank Enterprise Award Program	18	15
Native American CDFI Assistance	12	12
Bank on USA Program	NA	20
Total Budget Authority	$221	$221

Source: Community Development Financial Institutions Fund, *FY2013 President's Budget Submission*, Washington, DC, p.3, at http://www.treasury.gov/about/budget-performance/Documents/7%20-%20FY%202013%20CDFI%20CJ.pdf.
Note: Administration costs include administration of the New Markets Tax Credit.

CDFI and CDE Certification

To be eligible for certain Fund-related programs, an organization must be certified as either a CDFI or a Community Development Entity (CDE). CDFI certification is a designation conferred by the CDFI Fund and is a requirement for accessing financial award assistance from the CDFI Fund through the CDFI program, Native American CDFI Assistance (NACA) programs, and certain benefits under the Bank Enterprise Award (BEA) program to support an organization's established community development financing programs.

An organization that does not meet each of the certification eligibility requirements at the time of application for Technical Assistance is still eligible to apply for and receive Technical Assistance. This may occur if the Fund determines that the organization's application materials provide a realistic course of action to ensure that it will meet each of the certification requirements within two years of entering into an assistance agreement with the Fund.

A certified CDE is a domestic corporation or partnership that is an intermediary vehicle for the provision of loans, investments, or financial counseling in low-income communities (LICs).

CDE certification is required to receive an NMTC allocation. CDEs use the NMTC to encourage investors to make equity investments in the CDE or its subsidiaries.[11] **Table 2** provides the eligibility criteria for CDFI and CDE certification.

As of July 31, 2012, there were 999 certified CDFIs.[12] As shown in **Figure 1**, at least one CDFI is located in each of the 50 states, the District of Columbia, Guam, Puerto Rico, and the U.S. Virgin Islands. California and New York contain more certified CDFIs than any other U.S. state or territory.

Table 2. Eligibility Criteria for CDFI and CDE Certification

CDFI Certification	CDE Certification
• Be a legal entity • Have a primary mission of promoting community development • Primarily provide financial products, development services, or other similar financing in arms-length transactions • Primarily serve (direct at least 60% of financial product activities to) one or more geographic investment areas meeting certain poverty or income standards; low-income targeted populations; or other targeted populations that lack adequate access to capital and historically have been denied credit • Provide development services, such as credit or homebuying counseling, in conjunction with financial products • Maintain accountability to defined target markets through representation on governing or advisory board or through outreach activities • Be a nongovernment entity and not under control of any government entity (except tribal governments)	• Be a legal entity and a domestic corporation or partnership for federal tax purposes • Have a primary mission of serving or providing investment capital to low-income communities or low-income individuals and target at least 60% of activities to these groups • Maintain accountability to low-income communities through representation on governing or advisory board • Note: Certified CDFIs qualify as CDEs and only need to register as CDEs rather than apply for certification.

Source: Adopted from U.S. Government Accountability Office, *Community Development Financial Institutions and New Markets Tax Credit Programs in Metropolitan and Nonmetropolitan Areas*, GAO-12-547R, April 26, 2012, p. 4, at http://www.gao.gov/products/GAO-12-547R.

As of July 31, 2012, there were 5,780 certified CDEs (including their subsidiaries) located throughout the United States, Puerto Rico, and the U.S. Virgin Islands.[13] As shown in **Figure 2**, California and New York also contain more certified CDEs than any other U.S. state or territory.

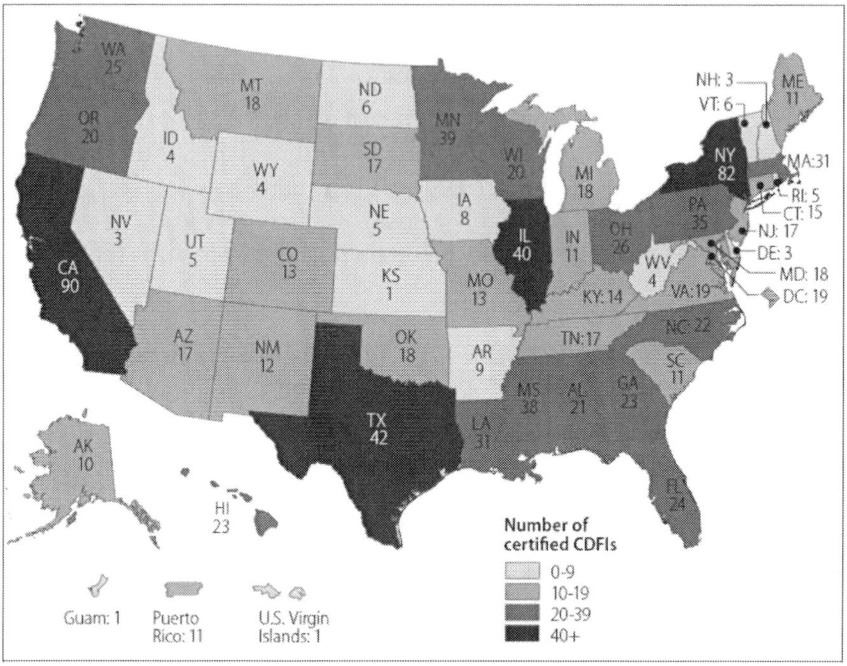

Source: Community Development Financial Institutions Fund, at http://www.cdfifund.gov/docs/certification/cdfi/CDFI%20List%20-%2007-31-12.xls.

Note: CDFI counts are as of July 31, 2012.

Figure 1. Certified CDFIs, by location.

PROGRAMS

The Fund's official mission is to increase economic opportunity and promote community development investments in low-income and distressed communities in the United States. To carry out this mission, the Fund is composed of several programs that address multiple needs of distressed communities. These programs encourage qualified entities to provide financial and technical assistance to meet the needs of local businesses, potential homebuyers, community developers, and potential investors in distressed and LICs. The Fund's range of incentives include equity investment in program awardees, tax credits, grants, loans, and deposits and credit union shares in insured CDFIs and state-insured credit unions.[14]

All of the Fund's programs share a common characteristic, in that they use geographically targeted incentives intended to increase community development in underserved and distressed communities, where certain types of economic activity might not otherwise occur. Ideas for geographically targeted community development policies were a feature of federal policy debates throughout the 1980s and early 1990s.[15] Despite bipartisan support for these policies at the time, they did not become more widely implemented, at the federal level, until the Clinton Administration.[16]

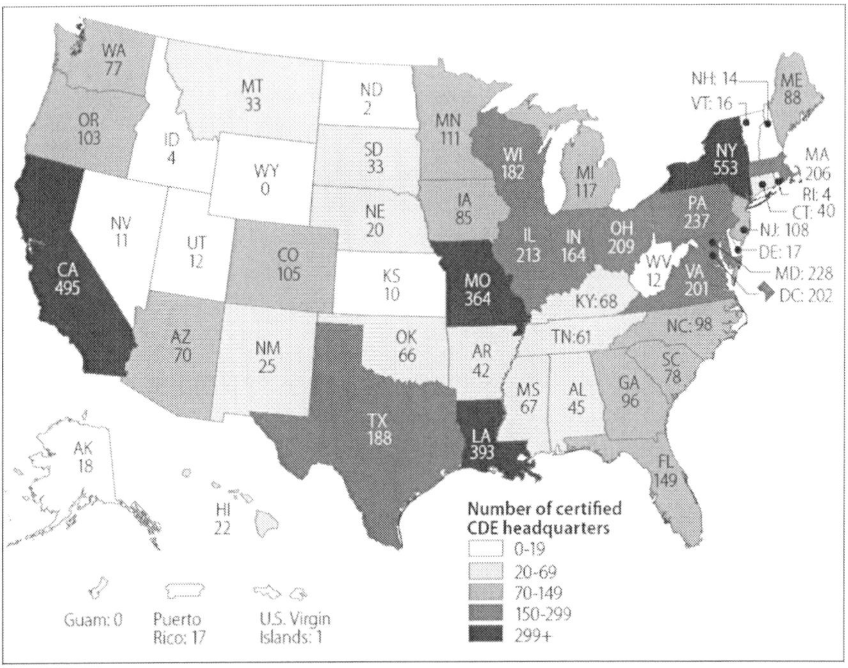

Source: Community Development Financial Institutions Fund, at http://www.cdfifund.gov/what_we_do/programs_id.asp?programID=10.

Note: CDE counts are as of July 31, 2012.

Figure 2. Certified CDEs, by location.

According to the Fund, it has awarded (as of the end of FY2010) $1.3 billion to CDFIs, community development organizations, and financial institutions through its core CDFI assistance program (and component initiatives) and the BEA program since the Fund's founding in 1994.[17] The Fund has also allocated $26 billion in tax credit authority to certified CDEs through the New Markets Tax Credit, between 2001 and 2010.

By the Fund's estimates, CDFIs that received the Fund's awards, in FY2011 alone, created or maintained more than 25,000 jobs, opened more than 6,500 bank accounts for the previously unbanked, and provided more than 177,000 individuals with financial literacy training.[18] The Fund's Community Investment Impact System, launched in 2004, contains these statistics gathered through reporting requirements that are part of the terms of each program's award agreements.[19]

CDFI Program

The Fund's core CDFI program was authorized by the Community Development Banking and Financial Institutions Act of 1994 in the Riegle Community Development and Regulatory Improvement Act of 1994 (P.L. 103-325). The CDFI program provides two types of monetary awards, financial assistance (FA) and technical assistance (TA). These awards are given to CDFIs to build their capacity of CDFIs to serve low-income people and communities that lack access to affordable financial products and services.[20]

To be eligible for an FA award, a CDFI must be certified by the Fund before it applies for the award. Prospective applicants that are not yet certified must submit a separate certification application to be considered for an FA award during a funding round. Both certified and non-certified CDFIs are eligible to apply for TA awards. However, non-certified organizations must be able to become certified within two years after receiving a TA award.

In evaluating and selecting applicants for awards, the Fund evaluates the applicants' likelihood of meeting its goals as described in a required comprehensive business plan. The applicants' prior history of servicing distressed communities, its operational capacity, financial track record, and other attributes are also taken into consideration.[21]

Activities eligible for program awards must target a *distressed community*, which is defined by two requirements. First, the community (investment area) must meet minimum area requirements. The community must be a continuous area of general local government that either has (1) a population of at least 4,000, if located in a Metropolitan Statistical Area, (2) a population of at least 1,000, in non-metropolitan areas, or (3) located entirely within an Indian reservation.[22]

Second, at least 30% of the eligible residents in the community must have incomes that are less than the national poverty level, as published by the U.S.

Bureau of Labor Statistics (BLS), and the community must have an unemployment rate that is at least 1.5 times greater than the national average, as determined by the BLS's most recent data. In addition, the Fund may specify other requirements in a program's applicable notice of funds availability (NOFA).[23] The Fund's online resource, CDFI Fund Mapping System (CIMS), designates which localities either fully qualify or partially qualify as distressed communities, based on the three criteria.[24]

If the community does not meet the individual minimum area requirements, the applicant may select two or more geographic units which, in the aggregate, meet the minimum area eligibility requirements, provided that none of the geographic units has a poverty rate less than 20%.[25]

Minimum Requirements for Meeting the CDFI Program's Definition of a Distressed Community:

- A contiguous area located with a unit of General Local Government with a population, as determined by the most recent census data available, of at least 4,000, if any of the portion of the area is located with a Metropolitan Area with a population of 50,000; a population of at least 1,000, in any other case; or be located entirely within an Indian reservation;
- At least 30% of the Eligible Residents have incomes that are less than the national poverty level, as published by the U.S. Bureau of the Census in the most recent decennial census for which data is available; the unemployment rate is at least 1.5 times greater than the national average, as determined by the U.S. Bureau of Labor Statistics' (BLS) most recent data, including estimates of unemployment developed using the BLS's Census Share calculation method; or
- Such additional requirements as may be specified by the Fund in the applicable notice of funds availability.

Source: 12 C.F.R. §1806.200(b).

The Fund makes awards up to $2 million to certified CDFIs under the FA component of the CDFI program.[26] A CDFI may use an FA award for lending, investing, enhancing liquidity, or other means of financing:

- commercial facilities that promote revitalization, community stability, or job creation or retention;

- businesses that provide jobs to, are owned by, or enhance the availability of products and services to low-income individuals;
- housing that is principally affordable to low-income persons, with some exceptions;
- the provision of consumer loans; or
- other businesses or activities as requested by the applicant and deemed appropriate by the Fund.[27]

The Fund awards grants of up $100,000 to certified CDFIs and established entities seeking to become certified under the TA component of the CDFI program.

TA awards are intended to build a CDFI's capacity to provide affordable financial products and services to low-income communities and families.[28] TA grants may be used for a variety of purposes, including

- the purchase equipment, materials, or supplies;
- to pay for consulting or contracting services;
- to pay the salaries and benefits of certain personnel;
- to train staff or board members;
- or other activities deemed appropriate by the Fund.[29]

FA and TA awards are both generally subject to two restrictions. First, the Fund typically requires an applicant to demonstrate that they can match from a non-federal source, dollar-for-dollar, the amount of money that they are requesting from the Fund.

With regard to FA awards, the Fund is authorized to make awards to applicants in a *like form* to the matching funds secured by the awardee.[30] For example, the Fund can only match a non-federal grant with an FA grant—not a loan. Second, the Fund generally limits any one entity or its affiliates from receiving more than $5 million in awards from the Fund within a three-year period.[31]

However, restrictions on the Fund's awards have been subject to temporary legislative changes. For example, the American Reinvestment and Recovery Act (ARRA) of 2009 (P.L. 111-5) waived the non-federal, dollar-for-dollar matching requirement for three years.[32] Thus, the Fund did not require awards in FY2009, FY2010, and FY2011 to be matched by non-federal sources.[33] The matching requirement returned for awards in FY2012 for Fund programs that did not receive a congressional wavier.[34] ARRA also waived the $5 million cap for FY2009, FY2010, and FY2011.[35]

Native American CDFI Assistance

The origin of the Native American CDFI Assistance (NACA) component of the CDFI program dates back to the Riegle Act of 1994. The Riegle Act mandated that the Fund conduct a study of lending and investment practices on Indian reservations. The study was directed to identify and determine the impact of private-financing barriers on Native American populations.[36] Since the November 2001 release of the Native American Lending Study, the Fund certifies Native CDFIs and provides assistance through the CDFI program's authority. These programs are designed to reduce barriers preventing access to credit, capital, and financial services in Native American, Alaska Native, and Native Hawaiian communities (collectively referred to as Native Communities).[37]

The Fund receives a separate appropriation for the NACA component of the CDFI program. Under the NACA component of the CDFI program, the Fund issues FA and TA awards to organizations with the primary mission of increasing access to capital in Native Communities. In addition, the NACA component provides TA grants to certified Native CDFIs, emerging Native CDFIs, and sponsoring entities (see below). TA awards may be used by the recipient to become certified as a Native CDFI or to create a new Native CDFI.

A CDFI must be certified by the Fund as one of three types of entities to become eligible for NACA's FA and TA awards:[38]

- *certified Native CDFI*, an organization must direct at least 50% of its activities toward serving Native Communities;
- *emerging Native CDFI*, an organization must demonstrate to the satisfaction of the Fund that is has a plan to achieve Native CDFI certification within a reasonable timeframe; or
- *sponsoring entity*, an organization (typically a tribe or tribal entity) must pledge that it will create a separate legal entity, which will eventually become certified as a Native CDFI.

For FY2012 funding rounds, Congress waived the matching funds requirement for FA applicants to the NACA program.[39]

Table B-1 summarizes the locations of Certified Native CDFIs, by state. Hawaii and Oklahoma contain more certified Native CDFIs than any other U.S. state.

As shown in **Table 1**, the Obama Administration requested $12 million for the assistance to Native CDFIs for FY2013.[40] Both the House and Senate

Committee on Appropriations also recommended $12 million in assistance for Native CDFIs for FY2013.[41]

Small and Emerging CDFI Assistance

The Small and Emerging CDFI Assistance (SECA) component of the CDFI program is designed to assist small or emerging CDFIs. It provides the same type of FA and TA awards as the general CDFI program. It distinguishes small or emerging CDFIs from other CDFIs using two eligibility criteria, as announced in the annual notice of funds availability. For FY2012 awards, a certified CDFI met the eligibility criteria of being a small or emerging CDFI if they had financial holdings below certain caps (based on their respective type of financial institution), or if they began operations after January 1, 2008.[42]

Awards provided through the SECA application are subject to caps on the size of the awards. For FY2012, these caps included $600,000 in general FA funds, up to and including $3.5 million funds under the FA funds designated for the Healthy Food Financing Initiative, and up to $100,000 in TA funds for capacity-building activities.[43] For FY2012 funding rounds, Congress waived the matching funds requirement for SECA program applicants.[44]

In FY2012, 26% of the total CDFI program applicant pool was requested by CDFIs that filed under the SECA component.[45]

Capacity Building Initiative

The Fund provides technical assistance and training opportunities for CDFIs through its Capacity Building Initiative. The Capacity Building Initiative is a combination of online and in-person resources.[46] The Fund's website provides a collection of best practices related to topics, such as microfinance operations, foreclosure intervention counseling, and healthy food retail financing in low-income communities. The Fund also offers a limited number of in-person training events on similar topics in different locations across the United States.

The Senate Committee on Appropriations recommended that $2 million of its $223 million in appropriations for the Fund be designated for the Capacity Building Initiative for FY2013.[47] The House Committee on Appropriations did not designate any level of funds specifically for the initiative.[48]

Healthy Food Financing Initiative

The Fund has used its authority within its CDFI program to support the Healthy Food Financing Initiative (HFFI), which began in FY2011. The Fund's HFFI is part of a multi-agency HFFI, involving Treasury, the U.S.

Department of Agriculture (USDA), and the U.S. Department of Health and Human Services (HHS).[49] The HFFI represents the federal government's effort to expand the supply and demand for nutritious foods, including increasing the distribution of agricultural products, developing and equipping grocery stores, and strengthening producer-to-consumer relationships. Through its role in the HFFI, the Fund provides grants for organizations serving low-income neighborhoods with limited access to affordable and nutritious food.

Congress appropriated $22 million for Fund activities related to the HFFI for FY2012. Twelve CDFIs focusing on developing solutions for increasing access to affordable healthy foods received grants in FY2011.[50] The Obama Administration and the Senate Committee on Appropriations recommended a $3 million increase (to $25 million) in FY2013 for the HFFI.[51] The House Committee on Appropriations did not recommend a specific level of funding for the HFFI for FY2013.[52]

New Markets Tax Credit

Congress established the New Markets Tax Credit (NMTC) program as part of the Community Renewal Tax Relief Act of 2000, contained within the Consolidated Appropriations Act, 2001 (P.L. 106-554),to encourage investors to make investments in impoverished, low-income communities (LICs) that traditionally lack access to capital. The NMTC is designed to increase private investment in LICs, where conventional access to credit and investment capital for developing small businesses, creating and retaining jobs, and revitalizing neighborhoods is often limited.[53] The NMTC is a non-refundable tax credit intended to encourage qualified investment groups to support community development entities (CDEs) that operate in eligible, LICs.[54] Although the NMTC is credited through the federal tax code, the Fund is responsible for awarding the tax credit allocations to eligible CDEs through a competitive award process. The credit provided to the investor totals 39% of the amount of the investment made in a CDE and is claimed over a seven-year credit allowance period.[55] In each of the first three years, the investor receives a credit equal to 5% of the total amount paid for the stock or capital interest at the time of purchase. For the final four years, the value of the credit is 6% annually. Investors must retain their interest in a qualified equity investment throughout the seven-year period, or risk forfeiture of that interest.[56]

Under the tax code's NMTC provisions, only eligible investments in qualifying LICs can receive the NMTC. Qualifying LICs include census tracts that have at least one of the following criteria: (1) a poverty rate of at least 20%; (2) is located in a metropolitan area, a median family income below 80% of the greater of the statewide, or metropolitan area median family income; or (3) if located outside a metropolitan area, a median family income below 80% of the median statewide family income. As defined by the criteria above, about 39% of the nation's census tracts covering nearly 36% of the U.S. population are eligible for the NMTC.[57] In addition, designated targeted populations may be treated as LICs. As a result of the definition of qualified LICs, virtually all of the country's census tracts are potentially eligible for the NMTC.[58]

Qualified investment groups can apply to the Fund for an allocation of the NMTC. CDEs seek individuals who can benefit from tax preferences to make qualifying equity investments in the CDE.[59] The CDE then makes equity investments in LICs and low-income community businesses, all of which must be qualified. After the CDE is awarded a tax credit allocation, the CDE is authorized to offer the tax credits to private equity investors in the CDE.

The Tax Relief, Unemployment Insurance Reauthorization, and Job Creation Act of 2010 (P.L. 111-312) extended NMTC authorization through 2011 at $3.5 billion per year. The 112th Congress may choose to reinstate the NMTC. The Family and Business Tax Cut Certainty Act of 2012 (S. 3521) would extend the NMTC for calendar years 2012 and 2013, with an allocation authority of $3.5 billion per year.[60] Despite a lack guaranteed appropriations of the NMTC for 2012, the Fund issued a notice of NTMC allocation availability for 2012 on July 24, 2012.[61]

The Government Accountability Office (GAO) has issued several reports examining the NMTC's overall performance and ability to benefit certain types of LICs. A 2007 GAO report contains survey results from a sample of NMTC recipients suggesting that the NMTC influenced the decisions of investors to invest in LICs.[62] GAO published a 2009 report responding to congressional concerns about the low success rate of minority-owned CDEs in obtaining NMTC allocations. GAO found that although a CDE's resources and experience are important factors in successfully obtaining an NMTC allocation, minority status is associated with a lower probability of receiving an allocation, when controlling for other factors. GAO could not determine why this relationship exists or whether any actions (or lack of) by the Department of the Treasury contributed to minority CDEs' lower probability of success, given that the Fund provides assistance that is available to all CDEs that do not receive awards detailing some of the weaknesses in its applications.[63] In a 2012 report, GAO concluded that although the NMTC directed most awards and tax credits to metropolitan areas, it generally met proportionality goals of nonmetropolitan areas.[64] Another GAO report released in 2012 reported that the effects of the NMTC are difficult to assess because of information gaps in the collection of tax data.[65]

In addition, the NMTC's complex application and administration have been the focus of GAO reports, which have provided recommendations to make the program simpler and more accessible to those in LICs. For example, a 2010 GAO report noted that the complexity of NMTC transaction structures appears to make it more difficult for CDEs to execute smaller transactions and results in less equity ending up in low-income community businesses than would likely end up there were the transaction structures simplified.[66] In a 2011 report, GAO suggested that Congress convert at least part of the NMTC to a grant program to increase the amount of federal subsidy reaching businesses in impoverished, LICs.[67]

Bank Enterprise Award

The Bank Enterprise Award (BEA) was originally authorized by the Bank Enterprise Act of 1991 in the Agriculture, Rural Development, Food and Drug Administration, and Related Agencies Appropriations Act, 1992 (P.L. 102-142). Prior to the creation of the Fund, the BEA was administered by the Comptroller of the Currency and the Federal Deposit Insurance Corporation (FDIC). Section 114 of the Riegle Community Development and Regulatory Improvement Act of 1994 (P.L. 103-325) moved the BEA under the operations of the Fund.

The Fund's BEA program provides formula-based grants to FDIC-insured banks and thrifts to expand investments in CDFIs and to increase lending, investment, and service activities within economically distressed communities. The Fund measures increases in an applicant's lending, investment, and service activities relative to a baseline of similar, qualified activities conducted by the applicant in the previous application cycle. BEA rewards are *retrospective*, awarding applicants for activities they have already completed, in contrast to the Fund's primary CDFI program—which typically award applicants based on their plans for the future.[68]

The BEA provides formula-based grants to qualified banks and thrifts based on three categories:

- *CDFI-related activities* include equity investments (e.g., grants, stock purchases, purchases of partnership interests, or limited liability company membership interests), equity-like loans, and support activities (e.g., loans, deposits, or technical assistance), to certified CDFIs.[69]

- *Distressed community financing activities* include loans or investments for home mortgages, housing development, home improvement, commercial real estate development, small businesses, and education financing in distressed communities.
- *Service activities* include the provision of financial services (e.g., check-cashing or money order services, electronic transfer accounts, and individual development accounts).[70]

FDIC-insured financial institutions that are dedicated to financing and supporting economic development in qualified communities are eligible for the BEA. No applicant may receive a BEA if it has (1) an application pending for assistance under the current round of the awards under the CDFI program; (2) been awarded assistance from the Fund under the CDFI program within the 12-month period prior to the date the Fund selects the applicant to receive a BEA; or (3) ever received assistance under the CDFI program for the same activities for which it is seeking a BEA.[71] Applicants may apply for both a CDFI program award and a BEA program award in a given year; however, receiving a CDFI program award removes an applicant from eligibility for a BEA in the same year.[72]

According to a GAO report, the Fund's authorizing statute places no restrictions on how BEA recipients may use their award.[73] In this same report, the Fund agreed with GAO's interpretation of its authorizing statute.[74] However, the Fund changed the terms of the program's award agreements in 2009.[75] Recipients must now use the award, or an amount equivalent to the award amount, for BEA qualified activities in a distressed community.[76] This change in the BEA program generated public requests for the Fund to provide further guidance on an awardee's reporting requirements.[77] As part of the BEA award agreement, the Fund now requires BEA recipients to account and track the use of the award (or an amount equivalent to the award amount) and verify that this amount was used in accordance with performance goals designated by the Fund.

As shown in **Table 1**, the Obama Administration recommended that the BEA program receive $15 million for FY2013.[78] Neither the House or Senate Committee on Appropriations recommended a specific level of funding for the BEA program for FY2013. The BEA program's effect on investment in distressed communities is the topic of multiple GAO reports to Congress.

In 1998, GAO reported that, according to the Fund, most of the 1996 awardees reported using their awards to further the objectives of the BEA program even though the program's authorizing legislation did not place restrictions on the use of the awards.[79] Each of GAO's five case study banks also reported using its award money to expand its existing investments in community development.[80] In a 2006 report, GAO concluded that the extent to which the BEA program may provide banks with incentives to increase their investments in CDFIs and lending in distressed communities is difficult to determine, but available evidence GAO reviewed suggested that the program's impact has likely not been significant. Award recipients GAO interviewed said that the BEA program lowers bank costs associated with investing in a CDFI or lending in a distressed community, allowing for increases in both types of activities. However, other economic and regulatory incentives also encourage banks to undertake award-eligible activities, and it is difficult to isolate and distinguish these incentives from those of a BEA award.[81] Treasury disputed GAO's findings and questioned GAO's methodology of evaluating the BEA program.

Bond Guarantee Program

The Small Business Jobs Act of 2010 (P.L. 111-240) authorized the Bond Guarantee program on September 27, 2010.[82] The Fund's Bond Guarantee program is designed to provide a low-cost source of long-term, patient capital to CDFIs.[83] Treasury may issue up to 10 bonds per year, each at a minimum of $100 million. The total of all bonds cannot exceed $1 billion per year. Each bond is fully guaranteed by the United States and offered at a cost equivalent to the current Treasury rates for comparable maturities. The bonds cannot exceed a maturity of 30 years, are taxable, and do not qualify for Community Reinvestment Act (CRA) credit.[84] Treasury guarantees the full amount of notes or bonds issued to support CDFIs that make investments for eligible community or economic development purposes.[85]

Authorized uses of the loans financed may include a variety of financial activities that constitute community or economic development in low-income or underserved areas (e.g., the provision of basic financial services, housing that is principally affordable to low-income individuals, and businesses that provide jobs for low-income people or are owned by low-income individuals).[86] By legislative design, the Bond Guarantee program is a zero subsidy credit program and does not require annual appropriations funding.

Since the bonds will be guaranteed by the United States, in accordance with federal credit policy, the Federal Financing Bank (FFB), a U.S. government corporation under the general supervision and direction of Treasury, will purchase the bonds issued by qualified issuers.[87] Qualified issuers will lend the bond proceeds to eligible CDFIs. The FFB finances obligations that are fully guaranteed by the United States, such as the bonds or notes issued by CDFIs under the CDFI Bond Guarantee Program.

The Fund has not yet published regulations concerning the eligibility criteria for its Bond Guarantee program, as of the publication date of this report.

Although the Bond Guarantee program is authorized through FY2014, it is awaiting further congressional authorization for its credit issuing authority. However, as a zero-subsidy federal program, the Bond Guarantee still requires specific authorization in the FY2013 appropriations bill to provide the initial round of bond guarantees.[88]

The Senate Committee on Appropriations has provided this authorization, but the House Committee on Appropriations has not.[89] Because the program is authorized to issue no more than $1 billion in bonds per year, delays in the program's potential lending ability, under current law, has been reduced from $4 billion to $2 billion between 2010 and 2014.

Bank on USA

In his FY2011 budget request, President Obama proposed the Bank on USA program as a means to facilitate access to, and evaluate the effectiveness of, affordable, high-quality financial products, services, and education to unbanked and underbanked individuals.[90] Title 12 of the Dodd-Frank Wall Street Reform and Consumer Protection Act (P.L. 111-203) authorized the Fund to "encourage initiatives for financial products and services that are appropriate and accessible for millions of Americans who are not fully incorporated into the financial mainstream."[91]

Although the President requested more than $41 million in funding for Bank on USA for FY2012, Congress did not approve funding for the program for FY2012.[92] The Obama Administration requested $20 million for the Fund's Bank on USA-related activities for FY2013.[93] The Senate Committee on Appropriations recommended $20 million for the Bank on USA program for FY2013, whereas the House Committee on Appropriations did not recommend a specific level of funds for the program for FY2013.[94]

POLICY CONSIDERATIONS

This section analyzes four policy considerations that may generate congressional attention, regarding the Fund's use of federal resources to promote economic development. First, it analyzes the debate on targeting development assistance toward people versus places. Second, it analyzes the debate over targeting economic development policies towards labor or capital. Third, it examines whether the Fund plays a unique role in promoting economic development, or if it duplicates, compliments, or competes with the goals and activities of other federal, state, and local programs. Fourth, it examines assessments of the Fund's management.

How Effective Are Geographically Targeted Economic Development Policies?

From an economic perspective, what theoretical basis is there for the promotion of development in distressed communities? Economic theory suggests that firms and workers will locate to the most efficient and productive areas to do business in the long run, without the assistance of government policy. From this perspective, government policies, such as tax exemptions or tax expenditures, that create incentives to locate in one area at the expense of another results in net social loss of efficiency—where finite resources are not being used to produce their maximum output for the lowest cost.[95] Economic theory indicates that these policies create a distortion in the market, such that resources are directed from an area of higher potential productivity to an area of lower potential productivity.[96]

However, government policy may be economically justified if business investment in distressed communities would generate positive *externalities*.[97] Positive externalities, also known as spillover benefits, occur when the actions of one individual or firm benefit others in society. Because a given business will tend to only consider its own (private) benefit from an activity, and not the total benefit to society, too little of the positive externality-generating activity may be undertaken from society's perspective. Governments, however, may intervene through the use of taxes, subsidies, and other forms of assistance to align the interests of individual businesses with the interests of society to achieve a more economically efficient outcome.

How may government policy generate positive externalities within a community? It is possible that potential investors may invest in an underdeveloped community as long as the potential return on that investment exceeds the potential risk. If investors are not attracted to a particular community, however, government incentives may be able to change investors' perceived return and risk calculations. If this initial group of businesses is successful, due in part to the government's incentives, then they may send positive signals about potential return for other businesses that choose to locate in the community. In addition, if government incentives encourage employment in the communities, employees may feel they have more of a stake in the community and participate positively in activities outside of work. Although government incentives initially benefit particular businesses or investments, they may also allow the broader community to capture these spillover benefits.

Empirical evaluations of geographically targeted economic development policies have been mixed.[98] Evaluations differ, in part, due to several factors, including the use of different evaluation criteria for economic development, different policies or sample areas used for analysis, or the use of different empirical strategies. Many of these studies are based on variations of state and local enterprise zones and federal empowerment zones. Enterprise zones typically provide certain tax incentives and regulatory relief for distressed communities, whereas federal Empowerment Zones provide certain tax exemptions and employer tax credits for hiring new employees.

Some studies have found that geographically targeted policies have a positive effect on several indicators of economic activity in the targeted area. These studies cite that these policies facilitate entrepreneurship and increase employment in the targeted area.[99]

Ham et al. find that Empowerment Zone designation reduces local unemployment and poverty rates by 8.7% and 8.8%, respectively, whereas enterprise zone designation reduces local unemployment and poverty rates by 2.6% and 20%, respectively.[100]

Papke's review of surveys from participants in multiple U.S. enterprise zones indicates that start-up firms average approximately 25% of new businesses within the targeted zones.[101] Rubin and Wilder's analysis of Indiana's Enterprise Zone indicates that 76% of the 1,878 jobs created between the beginning of the program in 1983 and 1986 could not be attributed to regional or sectoral growth.[102] Assuming that these residual jobs were created in large part due to policy, the researchers calculated that the creation of each of these 1,430 jobs cost taxpayers $1,372 per job, annually.[103]

On the other hand, other evaluations indicate that these policies have little effect on economic activity within the targeted area, or they do not contribute to a net increase of economic activity throughout the larger economy. These studies find that geographically targeted policies encourage some types of economic activity at the detriment of others—thus rearranging the mix of economic activity within the target area.[104] For example, Hanson and Rohlin indicate that location based-tax incentives have a positive effect on the firm location in industries that benefit the most from the tax incentives, but net growth in new establishments is offset by declines or slower growth in other industries that are less likely to utilize the tax incentives.[105]

In addition, some studies indicate that geographically targeted policies may shift activity from a comparative area toward the targeted zone, rather than create new economic activity. For example, Gurley-Calvez et al. find that the NMTC may have led to an increase in corporate investment within the targeted areas, but did not lead to a net increase in corporate investment.[106]

These authors conclude that the NMTC might encourage investment to shift from one low-income community (LIC) to another close substitute, as some corporate investors might already be investing in LICs to fulfill Community Reinvestment Act requirements.[107]

The effect of geographically targeted economic development policies on local property prices is also an area of contention among researchers.[108] From a theoretical perspective, government incentives to increase the supply of affordable property increase the demand for that property. That increase in demand drives rents higher. If local residents do not benefit from the increase in economic activity, then higher property values may encourage those with lower incomes to move out of the community.[109]

Given the lack of consensus among researchers on the effectiveness of geographically targeted economic policies, policymakers may opt to more narrowly define the core objective of *development*.

At its core, the debate is a question of whether development policies should help people or places. If the primary objective is to improve business and employment opportunities relative to other areas, then these policies might be effective. If the primary objective of such policies are to create new jobs, then the effect of these policies may be limited.

If policymakers wish to help the poor, then it might be asked why should government assistance only be extended to the poor living in distressed communities (as opposed to the poor living in non-distressed communities)? Each standard for evaluation implies a different set of metrics and results in a different set of trade-offs.

Should Economic Development Policies Target Capital or Labor?

Assuming that geographically targeted policies can positively affect economic development within the intended community, then what type of benefit is most effective? Policies can provide a benefit related to labor costs, capital costs, or both (i.e., total costs). In other words, should development policies target workers, business owners, or both? When a geographically targeted subsidy is applied to one of these two factors of production, economic theory suggests that two behavioral responses occur. The first response is that total output (i.e., economic activity) increases. This increase in total output increases the use of both capital and labor, to some degree. Economists label this the *output effect* of production. The second response is a substitution effect, whereby firms use one factor of production at the detriment of the other. The net effect of the output effect and *substitution effect* determines the total effect of the policy. In other words, the total effect reflects whether the policy benefits labor more than capital, or vice versa. For example, a labor subsidy, such as a payroll tax credit for hiring a worker, provided within a particular area will encourage labor-intensive firms to locate within that same area. All firms (whether attracted by the labor subsidy or already operating in the area) will tend, in addition to expanding operations, to substitute their use of labor for capital. If the objective of the labor subsidy is to promote employment, then the substitution effect (the use of more labor, relative to capital) reinforces the benefits of the output effect (the use of more labor, due to expanded operation). In other words, the policy is expected to result in a net increase in employment. By contrast, a capital subsidy, such as tax deductions for capital investments, provided within a particular area will encourage capital-intensive firms to locate within the area. All firms (whether attracted by the capital subsidy or already operating in the area) will tend, in addition to expanding operations, to substitute their use of capital for labor. If the objective of the capital subsidy is to promote employment, then the substitution effect (the use of more capital, relative to labor) offsets the benefits of the output effect (the use of more labor, due to expanded operation). Moreover, if the substitution effect is more powerful than the output effect, a capital subsidy may end up *decreasing* employment in the area.[110]

In this instance, the net effect of the capital subsidy is less employment in the area than before the policy. Policies that relate to total costs may balance the trade-off between the promotion of capital or labor in the targeted area.

If producers are indifferent between using labor or capital, then a policy that provides equally weighted incentives toward the employment of labor and capital will result in a positive income effect, with no substitution effect. However, if producers use relative factor price differentials to inform the mix of capital and labor they employ, then the result of a policy that relates to total costs will depend on the strength and direction of the substitution effect.

Studies indicate that geographically targeted tax incentives for business owners (e.g., the NMTC) have a positive, but limited effect in increasing the economic well-being of other individuals living within the target area. Bartik's review of 57 empirical studies on the effect of state and local preferential tax incentives for employers in a state or metropolitan area found that 57% of the studies found at least one statistically significant effect on generating development in the target area.[111] Bartik found that the average measure of responsiveness, or elasticities, or change between tax measures and economic activity in a targeted state or metropolitan area range from -0.25 across all studies to -0.51 for studies that include statistical controls for both public service and fixed effects. In other words, the study concluded that a 10% reduction in all taxes within a particular geographic zone would generate a 2.5% to 5.1% increase in economic activity within the same zone.

Do the Fund's Programs Duplicate Other Government Efforts?

There has been growing legislative interest in identifying duplicative federal programs, as some Members of Congress have become concerned about the size or efficient management of federal budgetary resources. GAO defines duplicative programs as federal programs that overlap with the goals or activities of other federal, state, or local policies.[112] Some say that the Fund's programs duplicate other federal, state, local, and private-sector efforts to increase economic development in distressed and low-income communities. The Fund's website contains a guide that provides a list of possible financing sources for CDFIs.[113] At the federal level, various programs exist as possible sources of finance for CDFIs.

These programs are managed by executive agencies, such as USDA, SBA, HHS, the Departments of Housing and Urban Development (HUD), Interior, Treasury, and Commerce. Based on this variety of possible funding sources for CDFIs, the Office of Management and Budget (OMB), under President George W. Bush, said that the Fund's core CDFI program was *not unique*, as several states administer similar programs and CDFIs can use private-sector equity investment to accomplish activities that they would otherwise accomplish with the Fund's awards.[114] In addition, the NMTC is not the only tax incentive designed to encourage economic development in distressed communities. The Senate Committee on the Budget Print on Tax Expenditures lists several other tax incentives that are meant to achieve similar goals as the NMTC. These incentives provide short-term development assistance (e.g., disaster relief provisions), enhance tribal area development, and encourage business and capital investment in target communities.[115] The Bush era's OMB also stated that the NMTC was not unique because other federal, state, and local tax credit programs are available through agencies, such as HUD and Commerce's Economic Development Agency.[116] On the other hand, there are those that believe that the Fund plays a unique or complementary role to the programs mentioned above. First, Fund supporters most commonly argue that community lenders are ready and willing to fill financing gaps, but they often struggle to find the amount of capital and liquidity they need to meet loan demand in distressed communities.[117]

Although certain CDFIs may be eligible for similar forms of assistance from other federal programs (e.g., guaranteed loans from SBA), the Fund's limitations to activities in distressed communities allows CDFIs to compete with other entities that face similar economic, environmental, and geographic challenges. Second, Fund programs have supported alternatives to predatory lending institutions in distressed communities—notably in tribal communities.[118] Third, some argue that the Fund's programs complement, not compete with, the goals and programs of other federal initiatives. For example, former-Assistant Secretary for Financial Institutions Michael Barr testified before the House Committee on Financial Services that funding for the Community Reinvestment Act encourages more entities to invest in CDFIs.[119]

In contrast to the assessment by the Bush era's OMB, some say that the Fund provides incentives for activity that private-sector investors would not otherwise engage in. For example, the Fund enables more CDFIs to provide affordable, critical-gap financing for businesses.[120] In other words, the Fund encourages CDFIs to provide short-term loans to businesses or homebuyers to cover financial obligations in the meantime, while that borrower secures sufficient funds to make a full payment or find a more stable financing scheme. In addition, CDFIs also provide technical assistance and training to borrowers to reduce default risk. For these reasons, some representatives from national banking chains argue that CDFIs complement traditional banking products in distressed and LICs and help these financial markets operate more efficiently.[121]

Is the Fund Managed Effectively?

Concerns over the Fund's management primarily involve questions over the transparency and consistency of the Fund's award evaluation processes. In March 1997, as a result of complaints about the selection process used in the first round of grants announced in July 1996, Representative Spencer Bachus, chairman of the General Oversight and Investigations Subcommittee (the Subcommittee) of the House Committee on Banking and Financial Services, requested information about management practices at the Fund from Treasury. At Chairman Bachus's request, the majority staff of the subcommittee published a report that reviewed the management practices at the Fund. The majority staff report indicated that the Fund had failed to employ an objective scoring system in selecting award winners in its first round of allocations, and that the director and deputy director of the Fund had participated in making awards to firms with that they had been previously associated.[122] Chairman Bachus asserted that the Fund's award evaluation process had been politically motivated by the White House, naming Shorebank of Chicago, Illinois, and several other community development organizations affiliated with Shorebank among the award-recipients.[123]

The majority staff report also indicated that, when it made its first round of awards, the Fund did not follow the recommendations of Treasury's Office of Inspector General (OIG) to adopt draft procedures for a numerical scoring system, a procedure similar to that used by other federal grant programs to ensure objectivity in the review process.[124] In August 1997, Treasury Secretary Robert Rubin replied to a request from Chairman Leach of the Senate Banking Committee by providing a detailed outline of procedural and organization reforms to be implemented by the Fund in its 1997 funding round.[125] These reforms included the development of selection criteria, a conflict of interest policy for Fund reviewers, and other tools and procedures to encourage consistent evaluation of award applications. Secretary Rubin's letter also announced the resignations of the Fund's director and deputy director. The subcommittee's staff conducted a review of the Fund's second round of awards in 1997. Although the majority staff report recommended further actions to enhance the fund's management and review processes, subcommittee staff concluded that the Fund "appeared to make great strides in documenting the grant process."[126] In addition, some have expressed concern about the Fund's ability to develop clear performance goals. In 1998, GAO released a report on the Fund's performance.[127] GAO acknowledged that assessing the Fund's performance was difficult, as the Fund's authorizing legislation provides limited guidance for evaluating performance measures and staffing limits delayed the Fund's ability to develop mandated monitoring and evaluation systems.[128] GAO stated that until the Fund identifies the types of data needed to monitor and evaluate awardees and incorporates these data needs in a formal system, it will be hampered in its ability to report on its progress toward achieving its stated goals and objectives.[129] GAO also noted that the Fund could fulfill its strategic goal to coordinate its strategies with other Treasury bureaus and agencies with similar missions (e.g., HUD and the SBA).[130] According to GAO, interagency coordination is important for ensuring that crosscutting programs are mutually reinforcing and efficiently implemented. Therefore, the Fund's strategic plan would be strengthened if it identified and incorporated some descriptions of other agencies' programs with similar missions and discussed their influence on the Fund's strategic objectives.[131] Some Members of Congress have expressed concern regarding the lack of CDFIs that serve U.S. territories and rural communities.[132] However, a 2012 GAO report concluded that the policies and procedures of the CDFI and NMTC Programs help ensure that awards and allocations generally are proportionate to the numbers of qualified applicants that serve metropolitan and nonmetropolitan areas.[133] In addition, some Members of Congress have expressed interest in the performance of CDFIs compared with their non-CDFI, peers.[134] In addition, some Members of Congress have raised concerns over the use of funds from the Troubled Asset Relief Program (TARP) for assistance to CDFIs. President Obama authorized a program that made certified CDFIs eligible to receive capital investments at a discounted dividend, with the intent of increasing the supply of credit to community banks.[135] Some maintained that TARP's temporary funds were not intended to target regional banks, and the program functionally resulted in a bypass of the typical appropriations process for the Fund.[136]

Appendix A. Inactive Programs

Capital Magnet Fund

The Housing and Economic Recovery Act (HERA) of 2008 (P.L. 110-289) established the Capital Magnet Fund (CMF) for CDFIs and other nonprofits to expand financing for the development, rehabilitation and purchase of affordable housing and economic development projects in distressed communities.[137] Through the CMF the Fund provided competitively awarded grants to CDFIs and qualified nonprofit housing organizations. CMF awards could be used to finance affordable housing activities as well as related economic development activities and community service facilities. Awardees were able to use financing tools, such as loan loss reserves, loan funds, risk-sharing loans, and loan guarantees, to produce eligible activities whose aggregate costs are at least 10 times the size of the award amount.[138]

Three types of organizations were eligible to apply for a CMF award. An organization applying for a CMF Award had to either (1) be certified as a CDFI by the Fund; (2) have an application for CDFI certification pending with the CDFI Fund, provided such application was submitted prior to the due date specified in the applicable notice of funds availability; or (3) be a nonprofit organization having as one of its principal purposes the development or management of affordable housing.[139] As authorized in HERA, CMF was to receive funding via a set-aside from government-sponsored enterprises (GSEs), such as Fannie Mae and Freddie Mac. However, such contributions have been suspended indefinitely. The GSEs never made contributions to the CMF, as was originally expected under HERA, due to their financial condition and status under conservatorships.[140] Instead, the Consolidation Appropriations Act, 2010 (P.L. 111-117) appropriated $80 million in initial funding for the CMF for FY2010.[141] Funding for the CMF was discontinued for FY2011.

The Fund awarded grants to 23 CDFIs and qualified nonprofit housing organizations serving in FY2010.[142] In FY2013, the Fund will provide performance results from the initial round of CMF recipients. The Fund received a total of 230 applications requesting $1 billion for the FY2010 CMF funding round.[143]

Financial Education and Counseling Pilot Program

The Financial Education and Counseling (FEC) pilot program provided grants through FY2010 to organizations that provided financial education and counseling services to prospective homebuyers. The goals of the FEC pilot program were to increase the financial knowledge and decision-making capabilities of prospective homebuyers, assist prospective buyers to plan for major purchases, and provide information on how to improve credit scores. Certified CDFIs, a HUD-approved housing counseling agency, credit union, or government entity could request FEC funding for administrative expenses for FEC-related programs.[144] Section 1132 of HERA of 2008 (P.L. 110-289) authorized the Secretary of the Treasury to create FEC pilot programs. For

FY2009, Congress appropriated $2 million to the Fund for the FEC program.[145] Treasury selected five organizations to receive $400,000 for their services toward the mission of the program.[146] In FY2010, Congress appropriated $4.15 million, of which $3.15 million was designated for an eligible organization in Hawaii.[147] A 2011 GAO report concluded that Treasury's process for selecting FEC grantees was applied consistently using established criteria. In 2010, the four grantees served a combined total of 311 clients.[148] However, GAO could not meaningfully assess the impact of the program or the effectiveness of individual grantees because grantees had been providing services under the FEC program for less than a year.[149]

APPENDIX B. CERTIFIED NATIVE CDFIS

Table B-1. Certified Native CDFIs, by State

State	Certified Native CDFIs
Hawaii	11
Oklahoma	10
Alaska	6
Arizona	6
South Dakota	6
Minnesota	5
Montana	4
California	3
Colorado	3
New Mexico	3
Washington	3
Wisconsin	3
Michigan	2
North Carolina	2
Maine	1
Mississippi	1
North Dakota	1
Oregon	1
Wyoming	1
Total	**72**

Source: Community Development Financial Institutions Fund, http://www.cdfifund.gov/docs/certification/cdfi/CDFI%20List%20-%2007-31-12.xls

Note: CDFI counts are as of July 31, 2012.

End Notes

[1] Ben S. Bernanke, "Community Banking," Speech at the Independent Community Bankers of America National Convention and Techworld, Nashville, TN, March 14, 2012, at http:// www.federalreserve.gov/newsevents/speech/ bernanke20120314a.htm.

[2] U.S. Congress, House Committee on Banking, Finance, and Urban Affairs, *Proposed Legislation: The Community Development Banking and Financial Institutions Act of 1993, Message from the President*, 103rd Cong., 1st sess., July 15, 1993, H. Doc. 103-118 (Washington: GPO, 1993).

[3] Ibid.

[4] The Emergency Supplemental Appropriations for Additional Disaster Assistance, for Anti-terrorism Initiatives, for Assistance in the Recovery from the Tragedy that Occurred at Oklahoma City, and Rescissions Act, 1995 (P.L. 104-19).

[5] See Lehn Benjamin, Julia Sass Rubin, and Sean Zielenbach, "Community Development Financial Institutions: Current Issues and Future Prospects," Proceedings, Board of Governors of the Federal Reserve System's Community Affairs Research Conference, *Sustainable Community Development: What Works, What Doesn't, and Why*, March 28, 2003, p. 7, at http://www.federalreserve.gov/communityaffairs/national/CA_Conf_ SusCommDev/pdf/zeilenbachsean.pdf.

[6] U.S. Department of the Treasury, "Organizational Structure," August 11, 2011, at http://www. treasury.gov/about/organizational-structure/Pages/default.aspx.

[7] Donna Gambrell was appointed to a three-year term as the Fund's director, which began in November 2007 and expired at the end of 2010. However, Ms. Gambrell has stayed on as director under Treasury's new rules.

[8] During the Clinton administration, funding was provided through the annual Veteran's Affairs-HUD-Independent agencies appropriations.

[9] Community Development Financial Institutions Fund, "Treasury Announces More Than $186 Million in Awards to Organizations Serving Low-Income and Native Communities," press release, August 6, 2012, at http://www.cdfifund.gov/%5Cnews_events%5CCDFI-2012-29-Treasury_Announces_More_Than_$186_Million_in_Awards_to_Organizations_Serving_L ow-Income_and_Native_Communities.asp.

[10] Community Development Financial Institutions Fund, *FY 2013 President's Budget Submission*, at http://www.treasury.gov/about/budget-performance/Documents/7%20-% 20FY%202013%20CDFI%20CJ.pdf.

[11] Community Development Financial Institutions Fund, "CDE Certification," at http://www. cdfifund.gov/what_we_do/programs_id.asp?programID=10.

[12] For a list of these certified CDFIs with their contact information, see Community Development Financial Institutions Fund, "CDFI Certification," at http://www.cdfifund.gov/what_we_ do/programs_id.asp?programID=9.

[13] For a list of these certified CDEs (and their subsidiaries) with their contact information, see Community Development Financial Institutions Fund, "CDE Certification," at http://www. cdfifund.gov/what_we_do/programs_id.asp?programID=10.

[14] 12 C.F.R. §1805.401.

[15] For a historical analysis of these debates, see the Discussion section of CRS Report R41268, *Small Business Administration HUBZone Program*, by Robert Jay Dilger.

[16] These programs include the 1993 reform of the Community Reinvestment Act of 1977 (P.L. 95-128) and the Empowerment Zone program, established by the Omnibus Budget Reconciliation Act of 1993 (P.L. 103-66).

[17] Community Development Financial Institutions Fund, *Performance and Accountability Report FY 2010*, , January 2011, p.4, at http://www.cdfifund.gov/docs/2011/cdfi/Performance-and-Accountabilty-Report-FY-2010.pdf.

[18] Community Development Financial Institutions Fund, *CDFI Program Awards FY 2012*, August 13, 2012, p. 6, at http://www.cdfifund.gov/docs/2012/cdfi/CDFI%20AWARDS book%208%202012.pdf.

[19] Community Development Financial Institutions Fund, "Research Reports, Research Briefs and Impact Data," May 5, 2012, at http://www.cdfifund.gov/impact_we_make/data_reports.asp.

[20] Laws pertaining to the Fund's FA and TA are located in 46 U.S.C. §§1805.300-1805.303.

[21] 12 CFR §1805.701.

[22] 12 C.F.R. §1806.200(b)(1).

[23] 12 C.F.R. §1806.200(b)(2).

[24] Community Development Financial Institutions Fund, "Community Development Financial Institutions Fund Mapping System (CIMS)," December 3, 2008, at http://www.cdfifund.gov/what_we_do/mapping.asp.

[25] 12 C.F.R. §1806.200(c).

[26] Community Development Financial Institutions Fund, "Community Development Financial Institutions Program," August 6, 2012, at http://www.cdfifund.gov/what_we_do/programs_id.asp?programid=7.

[27] 12 C.F.R. §1805.301.

[28] Ibid.

[29] 12 C.F.R. §1805.303.

[30] 12 C.F.R. §1805.501.

[31] 12 C.F.R. §1805.402(a). However, an entity and its affiliates may receive up to $8.75 million in awards from the Fund within a three year period if the entity serves an area where there are no other applicants for awards. These exceptions to $5 million cap are detailed in 12 C.F.R. §§1805.402(b)-(c).

[32] American Recovery and Reinvestment Act of 2009 (P.L. 111-5), 123 Stat. 148.

[33] Ibid.

[34] For FY 2012 funding rounds, Congress waived the matching funds requirement for Small and Emerging CDFI Assistance (SECA) program applicants and Financial Assistance (FA) applicants for the Native American CDFI Assistance (NACA) program. See Community Development Financial Institutions Fund, "Matching Funds Update for CDFI and NACA Program Applicants," press release, January 4, 2012, at http://www.cdfifund.gov/news_events/CDFI-2011-41-Matching_Funds_Funding_Cap_Update_CDFI_Program_NACA_Program_Applicants.asp.

[35] See Catalog of Federal Domestic Assistance, "Community Development Financial Institutions Program," program information, accessed August 13, 2012, at https://www.cfda.gov/?s=program&mode=form&tab=step1&id= 18dd106bf98422454e41f434ed2856d8.

[36] P.L. 103-325, Section 117(c).

[37] For the results of this study, see Community Development Financial Institutions Fund, *The Report of the Native American Lending Study*, November 2001, at http://www.cdfifund.gov/docs/2001_nacta_lending_study.pdf.

[38] Community Development Financial Institutions Fund, "Native American Initiatives Program," at http://www.cdfifund.gov/what_we_do/programs_id.asp?programid=3.

[39] Consolidated Appropriations Act, 2012 (P.L. 112-74), 125 Stat. 887.

[40] Community Development Financial Institutions Fund, *FY2013 President's Budget Submission*, , p.3, at http://www.treasury.gov/about/budget-performance/Documents/7%20-%20FY%202013%20CDFI%20CJ.pdf.

[41] U.S. Congress, House Committee on Appropriations, *Financial Services and General Government Appropriations Bill, 2013*, 112th Cong., 2nd sess., June 26, 2012, H.Rept. 112-550 (Washington: GPO, 2012), p. 16; and U.S. Congress, Senate Committee on Appropriations, *Financial Services and General Government Appropriations Bill, 2013*, 112th Cong., 2nd sess., June 14, 2012, S.Rept. 112-177 (Washington: GPO, 2012), p. 22.

[42] For FY2012, the caps for awards eligibility under SECA were set as follows: $250 million (insured depository institutions and depository institution holding companies), $10 million

(insured credit unions), $10 million (venture capital funds), and $5 million (other CDFIs). See Department of the Treasury, "Community Development Financial Institutions Fund - Funds Availability (NOFA) Inviting Applications for the Community Development Financial Institutions (CDFI) Program FY 2012 Funding Round," 76 *Federal Register* 68831-68841, November 7, 2011.

[43] Ibid.

[44] Consolidated Appropriations Act, 2012 (P.L. 112-74), 125 Stat. 887.

[45] Community Development Financial Institutions Fund, "Community Development Financial Institutions Fund Releases Application Demand for the FY 2012 CDFI Program Funding Round," press release, March 1, 2012, at http://www.cdfifund.gov/news_events/CDFI-2012-02-CDFI-Fund-Releases-Application-Demand-for-the-FY-2012-CDFI-Program-Funding-Round.asp.

[46] Community Development Financial Institutions Fund, "Capacity Building Initiative," March 25, 2010, at http://www.cdfifund.gov/what_we_do/programs_id.asp?programID=13.

[47] U.S. Congress, Senate Committee on Appropriations, *Financial Services and General Government Appropriations Bill, 2013*, 112th Cong., 2nd sess., June 14, 2012, S.Rept. 112-177 (Washington: GPO, 2012), p. 22.

[48] U.S. Congress, House Committee on Appropriations, *Financial Services and General Government Appropriations Bill, 2013*, 112th Cong., 2nd sess., June 26, 2012, H.Rept. 112-550 (Washington: GPO, 2012), p. 16.

[49] Community Development Financial Institutions Fund, "Community Development Financial Institutions Fund Announces $25 Million in Healthy Food Financing Initiative Awards," press release, September 14, 2011, at http://www.cdfifund.gov/news_events/CDFI-2011-18-CDFI-Fund-Announces-$25-Million-in-Healthy-Food-Financing-Initiative-Awards.asp.

[50] Community Development Financial Institutions Fund, "CDFI Fund Announces $25 Million in Healthy Food Financing Initiative Awards," press release, September 14, 2011, at http://www.cdfifund.gov/news_events/CDFI-2011-18-CDFI-Fund-Announces-$25-Million-in-Healthy-Food-Financing-Initiative-Awards.asp.

[51] U.S. Congress, Senate Committee on Appropriations, *Financial Services and General Government Appropriations Bill, 2013*, 112th Cong., 2nd sess., June 14, 2012, S.Rept. 112-177 (Washington: GPO, 2012), p. 22.

[52] U.S. Congress, House Committee on Appropriations, *Financial Services and General Government Appropriations Bill, 2013*, 112th Cong., 2nd sess., June 26, 2012, H.Rept. 112-550 (Washington: GPO, 2012), p. 16.

[53] U.S. Government Accountability Office, *New Markets Tax Credit: The Credit Helps Fund a Variety of Projects in Low-Income Communities, but Could Be Simplified*, GAO-10-334, January 2010, p. 1, at http://www.gao.gov/new.items/d10334.pdf.

[54] A non-refundable tax credit, like the NMTC, can be used to reduce tax liability toward, but not below, zero. In contrast, a refundable tax credit can be used to reduce tax liability beyond zero, enabling a taxpayer to receive a tax refund from the Internal Revenue Service.

[55] Laws pertaining to the NMTC are located in 26 U.S.C. §45D.

[56] For more details on the NMTC, see CRS Report RL34402, *New Markets Tax Credit: An Introduction*, by Donald J. Marples.

[57] CRS Report RL34402, *New Markets Tax Credit: An Introduction*, by Donald J. Marples.

[58] Ibid.

[59] If an investor does not have a tax liability, then the investor would not benefit from the non-refundable NMTC.

[60] Joint Committee on Taxation, *Description of the "Family and Business Tax Cut Certainty Act of 2012"*, JCX-67-12, July 31, 2012, at http://www.finance.senate.gov/legislation/download/?id=33b9fd68-7a66-4875-a069-0d74f874bad6.

[61] Department of the Treasury, "Community Development Institutions Fund - Funding Opportunity Title: Notice of Allocation Availability (NOAA) Inviting Applications for the

CY 2012 Allocation Round of the New Markets Tax Credit (NMTC) Program," 77 *Federal Register* 142, July 24, 2012.

[62] U.S. Government Accountability Office, New Markets Tax Credit Appears to Increase Investment by Investors in Low-Income Communities, but Opportunities Exist to Better Monitor Compliance, GAO-07-296, January 2007, p. 35, at http://www.gao.gov/new.items/ d07296.pdf.

[63] U.S. Government Accountability Office, *New Markets Tax Credit: Minority Entities Are Less Successful in Obtaining Awards Than Non-Minority Entities*, GAO-09-536, April 2009, at http://www.gao.gov/new.items/ d09536.pdf.

[64] U.S. Government Accountability Office, *Community Development Financial Institutions and New Markets Tax Credit Programs in Metropolitan and Nonmetropolitan Areas*, GAO-12-547R, April 2012, at http://www.gao.gov/ assets/600/590432.pdf.

[65] U.S. Government Accountability Office, *Limited Information on the Use and Effectiveness of Tax Expenditures Could be Mitigated Through Congressional Action*, GAO-12-262, February 2012, at http://gao.gov/assets/590/ 588978.pdf.

[66] See U.S. Government Accountability Office, *New Markets Tax Credit: The Credit Helps Fund a Variety of Projects in Low-Income Communities, but Could Be Simplified*, GAO-10-334, January 2010, p.41, at http://www.gao.gov/new.items/d10334.pdf.

[67] U.S. Government Accountability Office, *Opportunities to Reduce Potential Duplication of Government Programs, Save Tax Dollars, and Enhance Revenue*, GAO-11-318SP, March 2011, at http://www.gao.gov/new.items/ d11318sp.pdf.

[68] The Fund publishes a more in-depth account of its BEA application evaluation process regularly in the program's notice of funds availability. For example, see Department of Treasury, "Community Development Financial Institutions Fund - Notice of Funds Availability (NOFA) inviting Applications for the FY 2012 Funding Round of the Bank Enterprise Award (BEA) Program," 77 *Federal Register* 37742-37749, June 22, 2012.

[69] Community Development Financial Institutions Fund, "FY 2012 Funding Round of BEA Program Now Open," press release, June 30, 2012, at http://www.cdfifund.gov/news_ events/CDFI-2012-24-FY_2012_Funding_Round_of_BEA_Program_Now_Open.asp.

[70] 12 C.F.R. §1806.101(3)(c).

[71] 12 C.F.R. §1805.102, and U.S. Department of the Treasury, "Community Development Financial Institutions Fund - Notice of Funds Availability (NOFA) inviting Applications for the FY 2012 Funding Round of the Bank Enterprise Award (BEA) Program," 77 *Federal Register* 37743, June 22, 2012.

[72] Ibid.

[73] U.S. Government Accountability Office, Treasury's Bank Enterprise Award Program: Impact on Investments in Distressed Communities Is Difficult to Determine, but Likely Not Significant, GAO-06-824, July 2006, p. 6, at http://www.gao.gov/new.items/d06824.pdf.

[74] Ibid., p.28.

[75] Department of the Treasury, "Community Development Financial Institutions Fund 12 CFR Part 1806," 74 *Federal Register* 5790, January 30, 2009.

[76] 12 C.F.R. §1806.101(c).

[77] Letter from Joseph Pigg, Vice President and Senior Counsel, to Jodie Harris, Associate Program Manager - Community Development Financial Institutions Fund, March 24, 2010, at http://www.aba.com/Issues/Documents/c7e6303e475b4085afef85855eb422f632410 TreasuryBankEnterpriseAwardProgramBEA.pdf.

[78] Community Development Financial Institutions Fund, *FY2013 President's Budget Submission*, p. 3, athttp://www.treasury.gov/about/budget-performance/Documents/7%20-%20FY% 202013%20CDFI%20CJ.pdf.

[79] Ibid.

[80] Ibid., p.54.

[81] See U.S. Government Accountability Office 1998, and U.S. Government Accountability Office, Treasury's Bank Enterprise Award Program: Impact on Investments in Distressed

Communities is Difficult to Determine, but Likely Not Significant, GAO-06-824, July 2006, p. 4, at http://www.gao.gov/new.items/d06824.pdf.

[82] Laws pertaining to the Fund's Bond Guarantee program are located in 12 U.S.C. §4713a.

[83] Patient capital refers to an investment in which the investor has little expectation of earning a short-term return, in anticipation of earning more substantial returns in the longer-run.

[84] Community Development Financial Institutions Fund, "CDFI Bond Guarantee Program," at http://www.cdfifund.gov/what_we_do/programs_id.asp?programID=14.

[85] Ibid.

[86] Ibid.

[87] Catalog of Federal Domestic Assistance, "Community Development Financial Institutions Bond Guarantee Program," at https://www.cfda.gov/?s=program&mode=form&tab=step1&id=90977a236dc41c64b428744a8180642b.

[88] Any federal program that provides direct loans or loan guarantees is subject to Federal Credit Reform Act (FCRA) of 1990 in the Omnibus Budget Reconciliation Act of 1990 (P.L. 101-508). Sections 504 and 505 of FCRA require an annual appropriations bill to provide budget authority for new direct loan obligations incurred during the relevant fiscal year. For more information, see CRS Report R42632, *Budgetary Treatment of Federal Credit (Direct Loans and Loan Guarantees): Concepts, History, and Issues for the 112th Congress*, by James M. Bickley.

[89] U.S. Congress, House Committee on Appropriations, Financial Services and General Government Appropriations Bill, 2013, 112th Cong., 2nd sess., June 26, 2012, H.Rept. 112-550 (Washington: GPO, 2012), p. 16.; and U.S. Congress, Senate Committee on Appropriations, Financial Services and General Government Appropriations Bill, 2013, 112th Cong., 2nd sess., June 14, 2012, S.Rept. 112-177 (Washington: GPO, 2012), p. 22.

[90] Community Development Financial Institutions Fund, *FY2013 President's Budget Submission*, , p. 9, at http://www.treasury.gov/about/budget-performance/Documents/7%20-%20FY%202013%20CDFI%20CJ.pdf.

[91] Community Development Financial Institutions Fund, *FY 2013 President's Budget Submission*, p.12, at http://www.treasury.gov/about/budget-performance/Documents/7%20-%20FY%202013%20CDFI%20CJ.pdf.

[92] Ibid., p. 11.

[93] Ibid., p. 9.

[94] U.S. Congress, House Committee on Appropriations, Financial Services and General Government Appropriations Bill, 2013, 112th Cong., 2nd sess., June 26, 2012, H.Rept. 112-550 (Washington: GPO, 2012), p. 16.; and U.S. Congress, Senate Committee on Appropriations, Financial Services and General Government Appropriations Bill, 2013, 112th Cong., 2nd sess., June 14, 2012, S.Rept. 112-177 (Washington: GPO, 2012), p. 22.

[95] Economists typically view the most efficient means of production as the one that provides the most benefit at the lowest cost.

[96] Herbert G. Grubel, "Review of *Enterprise Zones: Greenlining the Inner Cities,* by Stuart M. Butler," *Journal of Economic Literature*, vol. XX (December 1982), pp. 1614-1616.

[97] A non-economic justification for a governmental role in targeted economic development policy is that these low-income communities are largely composed of minority or low-education populations. Although this argument is outside of the scope of this paper, more information on this policy justification can be found in Timothy Bartik, *Who Benefits From State and Local Economic Development Policies?* (Kalamazoo, MI: W. E. Upjohn Institute for Employment Research, 1991).

[98] Terry F. Buss, "The Effect of State Tax Incentives on Economic Growth and Firm Location Decisions: An Overview of the Literature," *Economic Development Quarterly*, vol. 15, no. 1 (February 2001), pp. 90-105.

[99] For other studies that have found that geographically targeted development policies have positive effects on economic activity in the target area, see Stephen Billings, "Do Enterprise Zones Work? An Analysis at the Borders," *Public Finance Review*, vol. 37, no. 1 (2008),

pp. 68-93, and Douglas Krupka and Douglas Noonan, "Empowerment Zones, Neighborhood Change, and Owner Occupied Housing," *Regional Science and Urban Economics*, vol. 39, no. 4 (2009), pp. 386-396.

[100] John C. Ham et al., "Government Programs Can Improve Local Labor Markets: Evidence from State Enterprise Zones, Federal Empowerment Zones, and Federal Enterprise Communities," *Journal of Public Economics*, vol. 95, no.7-8 (July 2011), pp. 779-797.

[101] Leslie Papke, "What Do We Know About Enterprise Zones?," in *Tax Policy and the Economy*, ed. James Poterba, vol. 7 (Cambridge, MA: MIT Press, 1993), pp. 32-72.

[102] Barry M. Rubin and Margaret G. Wilder, "Urban Enterprise Zones: Employment Impacts and Fiscal Incentives," *Journal of the American Planning Association*, vol. 55, no. 4 (Autumn 1989), pp. 418-431.

[103] Rubin and Wilder's cost estimates are among the lowest in the literature. In Ladd's review of six studies of enterprise zones, the basic annual cost estimates of various programs ranged from $1,633 to $53,507 per job, depending on methodology used to calculate costs. Bartik's (1992) review of 57 studies of state and local tax incentives found annual cost estimates ranging from $2,000 to $11,000 per job. See Helen F. Ladd, "Spatially Targeted Economic Development Strategies: Do They Work?," *Cityscape*, vol. 1, no. 1 (August 1994), pp. 193-218, and Timothy J. Bartik, "The Effects of State and Local Taxes on Economic Development: A Review of Recent Research," *Economic Development Quarterly*, vol. 6, no. 1 (1992), pp. 102-111.

[104] For studies that have found that geographically targeted development policies have little or no positive effects on economic activity in the target area, see Marlon Boarnet and William Bogart, "Enterprise Zones and Employment: Evidence from New Jersey," *Journal of Urban Economics*, vol. 40, no. 2 (1996), pp. 198-215; Danielle Bondonio and John Engberg, "Enterprise Zones and Local Employment: Evidence from the States' Programs," *Regional Science and Urban Economics*, vol. 30, no. 5 (2000), pp. 519-549; Robert Greenbaum and John Engberg, "The Impact of State Enterprise Zones on Urban Manufacturing Establishments," *Journal of Policy Analysis and Management*, vol. 23, no. 2 (2004), pp. 315-339; and David Neumark and Jed Kolko, "Do Enterprise Zones Create Jobs? Evidence from California's Enterprise Zone Program," *Journal of Urban Economics*, vol. 68, no. 1 (2010), pp. 1-19.

[105] Andrew Hanson and Shawn Rohlin, "Do Location-Based Tax Incentives Attract New Business Establishments?," *Journal of Regional Science*, vol. 51, no. 3 (2011), pp. 427-449.

[106] Tami Gurley-Calvez et al., "An Analysis of the New Markets Tax Credit," *Public Finance Review*, vol. 37, no. 4 (July 2009), pp. 371-398.

[107] The Community Reinvestment Act (CRA), passed by Congress in 1977, encourages financial institutions to help meet their communities' needs through safe and sound lending practices and by providing retail banking and community development services. The Federal Reserve System, the Federal Deposit Insurance Corporation, the Office of the Comptroller of the Currency, and the Office of Thrift Supervision are responsible for enforcing the CRA. Banksare evaluated for their CRA performance according to various criteria. See Federal Reserve Bank of Atlanta, "Standards Used to Evaluate Your Bank's CRA Performance," at http://www.frbatlanta.org/pubs/cra/standards_used_to_evaluate_your_banks_cra_performance.cfm.

[108] For studies that have model the effects of geographically targeted development policies on property values in the target area, see Douglas Krupka and Douglas Noonan, "Empowerment Zones, Neighborhood Change, and Owner Occupied Housing," *Regional Science and Urban Economics*, vol. 39, no. 4 (2009), pp. 386-396 and Andrew Hanson, "Local Employment, Poverty, and Property Value Effects of Geographically-Targeted Tax Incentives: An Instrumental Variables Approach," *Regional Science and Urban Economics*, vol. 39, no. 6 (November 2009), pp. 721-731.

[109] Andrew Hanson and Shawn Rohlin, "The Effect of Location Based Tax Incentives on Establishment Location and Employment Across Industry Sectors," *Public Finance Review*, vol. 39, no. 2 (March 2011), pp. 195-225.

[110] CRS Report 92-476 S *Enterprise Zones: The Design of Tax Incentives*, by Jane G. Gravelle (out of print; available by request) models this possible effect of geographically targeted tax incentives.

[111] Bartik (1992).

[112] U.S. Government Accountability Office, *Opportunities to Reduce Duplication, Overlap and Fragmentation, Achieve Savings, and Enhance Revenue*, GAO-12-342SP, February 28, 2012, p.1, http://www.gao.gov/products/GAO-12-342SP.

[113] Community Development Financial Institutions Fund, *Financial Resources Catalog*, June 11, 2012, at http://www.cdfifund.gov/what_we_do/resources/Financial%20Resources%20 Catalogue%20PDF.pdf.

[114] The Office of Management and Budget (OMB) under President George W. Bush maintained ExpectMore.gov, a website that listed performance evaluations and issued budgetary recommendations across executive branch agencies. OMB under President Bush implemented the Program Assessment Rating Tool (PART), as a means to assess the effectiveness of federal programs and help inform management actions, budget requests, and legislative proposals. For OMB's last PART assessment of the Fund and the NMTC, see Office of Management and Budget, *FY 2009 Budget Performance: Community Development Financial Institutions Fund*, pp. 15-16, at http://www.treasury.gov/about/ budget-performance/Documents/CJ%20FY09-CDFI.pdf.

[115] See U.S. Congress, Senate Committee on the Budget, *Tax Expenditures: Compendium of Background Material on Individual Provisions*, committee print, prepared by the Congressional Research Service, 111th Cong., 2nd sess., December 2010, S.Prt.111-58 (Washington: GPO, 2002), pp. 566-599.

[116] Office of Management and Budget, *FY 2009 Budget Performance: Community Development Financial Institutions Fund*, pp. 15-16, at http://www.treasury.gov/about/budget-performance/Documents/CJ%20FY09-CDFI.pdf.

[117] U.S. Congress, House Committee on Financial Services, *Community Development Financial Institutions (CDFIs): Their Unique Role and Challenges Serving Lower-Income, Underserved, and Minority Communities*, 111th Cong., 2nd sess., March 9, 2010, 111-106 (Washington: GPO, 2010), p.99.

[118] U.S. Congress, Senate Committee on Indian Affairs, *Predatory Lending in Indian Country*, 110th Cong., 2nd sess., June 5, 2008, 110-484 (Washington: GPO, 2008), p. 13.

[119] U.S. Congress, House Committee on Financial Services, *Community Development Financial Institutions (CDFIs): Their Unique Role and Challenges Serving Lower-Income, Underserved, and Minority Communities*, 111th Cong., 2nd sess., March 9, 2010, 111-106 (Washington: GPO, 2010), p.7.

[120] Federal Reserve Bank of Richmond, "Community Development Financial Institutions: A Unique Partnership for Banks," *Community Development Special Issue*, 2011, p.2, at http:// www.richmondfed.org/community_development/announcements/2011/pdf/cdfi-special-2011.pdf.

[121] Ibid.

[122] U.S. Congress, House Committee on Banking and Financial Services, Subcommittee on General Oversight and Investigations, *Review of Management Practice at the Treasury Department's Community Development Financial Institutions Fund*, committee print, prepared by Majority Staff, 105th Cong., 2nd sess., June 1998, 105-2 (Washington: GPO, 1998), pp. 1-9.

[123] Ibid., p. (v) and 9. Note 1 on p. 9 details the majority staff's views on the connections between Shorebank, its affiliates, First Lady Hillary Clinton, and President Clinton.

[124] Ibid., p. 4.

[125] Ibid., p. 95.

[126] Ibid., p. 96.

[127] Section 112(c)(3) of the Riegle Act mandated the Comptroller General (Director of GAO) to submit to the President and the Congress a study evaluating the structure, governance, and performance of the Fund. However, GAO, in consultation with the four congressional committees that the report was submitted to, only examined the Fund's performance measures in its 1998 study, due to a concurrent audit of structure and governance issues being conducted by Treasury's Inspector General. See the correspondence of Judy A. England-Joseph, GAO Director of Housing and Community Development Issues to Congressional Committees in U.S. General Accounting Office, *Community Development Financial Institutions Fund Can Improve Its Systems to Measure, Monitor, and Evaluate Awardees' Performance*, GAO/RCED-98-225, July 1998, at http://www.gao.gov/assets/160/156245.pdf.

[128] Ibid., p.6.

[129] Ibid., p.63.

[130] Ibid., p.62.

[131] Ibid.

[132] U.S. Congress, House Committee on Appropriations, *Financial Services and General Government Appropriations Bill, 2013*, 112th Cong., 2nd sess., June 26, 2012, H.Rept. 112-550 (Washington: GPO, 2012), p. 16.

[133] U.S. Government Accountability Office, *Community Development Financial Institutions and New Markets Tax Credit Programs in Metropolitan and Nonmetropolitan Areas*, GAO-12-547R, April 26, 2012, p. 4,http://www.gao.gov/assets/600/590432.pdf.

[134] U.S. Congress, House Committee on Financial Services, *Community Development Financial Institutions (CDFIs): Their Unique Role and Challenges Serving Lower-Income, Underserved, and Minority Communities*, 111th Cong., 2nd sess., March 9, 2010, 111-106 (Washington: GPO, 2010), p. 19 and 24.

[135] U.S. Department of the Treasury, "Obama Administration Announces Enhancements for TARP Initiative for Community Development Financial Institutions," press release, February 3, 2010, at http://www.cdfifund.gov/docs/ 2010/cdfi/Obama-Administration-Announces-Enhancements-Tarp-Initiative-for-Community-Dev-Fin-Inst.pdf.

[136] U.S. Congress, House Committee on Financial Services, *Community Development Financial Institutions (CDFIs): Their Unique Role and Challenges Serving Lower-Income, Underserved, and Minority Communities*, 111th Cong., 2nd sess., March 9, 2010, 111-106 (Washington: GPO, 2010), p. 8.

[137] Laws pertaining to the CMF are located in 46 U.S.C. §1807.

[138] Community Development Financial Institutions Fund, "Capital Magnet Fund," June 8, 2012, at http://www.cdfifund.gov/what_we_do/programs_id.asp?programID=11.

[139] Ibid.

[140] U.S. Congress, House Committee on Financial Services, Subcommittee on Capital Markets and Government Sponsored Enterprises, *Transparency, Transition, and Taxpayer Protection: More Steps to End the GSE Bailout*, 112th Cong., 1st sess., May 25, 2011, 112-33 (Washington: GPO, 2011), p. 10.

[141] Department of the Treasury, *Community Development Financial Institutions Fund - Agency Financial Report FY2011*, November 16, 2011, p. 8, at http://www.cdfifund.gov/news_events/CDFI%20Fund%20FY%202011%20Agency%20Financial%20Report%20FINAL%2011%2016%2011.pdf.

[142] U.S. Department of the Treasury, *Community Development Financial Institutions Fund: Agency Financial Report FY 2012*, November 2011, at http://www.cdfifund.gov/news_events/CDFI%20Fund%20FY%202011%20Agency%20Financial%20Report%20FINAL%2011%2016%2011.pdf.

[143] Department of the Treasury, *Community Development Financial Institutions Fund - Agency Financial Report FY2011*, November 16, 2011, p. 30, at http://www.cdfifund.gov/news_

events/CDFI%20Fund%20FY%202011%20Agency%20Financial%20Report%20FINAL%2011%2016%2011.pdf.

[144] For further details about the objective and eligibility criteria of the FEC pilot program, see Community Development Financial Institutions Fund, "Financial Education and Counseling Pilot Program," June 5, 2012, at http://www.cdfifund.gov/what_we_do/programs_id.asp?programID=8.

[145] U..S. Department of Treasury Office of Inspector General, *Audit of the Community Development Financial Institutions Fund's Fiscal Years 2010 and 2009 Financial Statements*, Department of the Treasury, OIG-11-024, November 15, 2010, at http://www.treasury.gov/about/organizational-structure/ig/Documents/oig11024%20%28CDFI%20Financials%20FY%2010%29.pdf.

[146] U.S. Government Accountability Office, *Financial Education and Counseling*, GAO-11-737R, July 27, 2011, p.2, at http://www.gao.gov/new.items/d11737r.pdf.

[147] Ibid.

[148] According to the 2011 GAO report, one grantee, the New Hampshire Housing Finance Authority, used their FEC award to develop an interactive financial education website that had not been launched when GAO reports were due.

[149] Ibid.

In: The Community Development ... ISBN: 978-1-62417-551-0
Editor: Andre L. Wright

Chapter 2

NEW MARKETS TAX CREDIT: AN INTRODUCTION*

Donald J. Marples

SUMMARY

The New Markets Tax Credit (NMTC) is a non-refundable tax credit intended to encourage private capital investment in eligible, impoverished, low-income communities. NMTCs are allocated by the Community Development Financial Institutions Fund (CDFI), a bureau within the United States Department of the Treasury, under a competitive application process. Investors who make qualified equity investments reduce their federal income tax liability by claiming the credit. The NMTC program, enacted in 2000, is currently authorized to allocate $33 billion through the end of 2011. To date, the CDFI has exhausted through 664 awards totaling $33 billion in NMTC's allocation authority.

The 111th Congress extended and modified the NMTC program authorization. The American Recovery and Reinvestment Tax Act of 2009, P.L. 111-5, increased the NMTC allocation for 2008 and 2009 to $5 billion from $3.5 billion. Further, the Tax Relief, Unemployment Insurance Reauthorization, and Job Creation Act of 2010 (P.L. 111-312) extended the NMTC authorization through 2011 at $3.5 billion per year.

* This is an edited, reformatted and augmented version of the Congressional Research Service Publication, CRS Report for Congress RL34402, dated March 7, 2012.

In the 112th Congress H.R. 2655 and H.R. 3224 would both extend the NMTC through 2016 with allocation authority of $5 billion $10 billion, respectively.

Overview

The New Markets Tax Credit (NMTC) was enacted by the Community Renewal Tax Relief Act of 2000 (P.L. 106-554) to provide an incentive to stimulate investment in low-income communities (LIC). The original allocation authority eligible for the NMTC program was $15 billion from 2001 to 2007.[1]

Congress, subsequently, has increased the total allocation authority to $33 billion and extended the program through 2011.[2] Qualified investment groups apply to the U.S. Department of the Treasury's Community Development Financial Institutions Fund (CDFI) for an allocation of the New Markets Tax Credit. The investment group, known as a Community Development Entity (CDE), seeks taxpayers to make qualifying equity investments in the CDE. The CDE then makes equity investments in low-income communities and low-income community businesses, all of which must be qualified. After the CDE is awarded a tax credit allocation, the CDE is authorized to offer the tax credits to private equity investors in the CDE.

The tax credit value is 39% of the cost of the qualified equity investment and is claimed over a seven-year credit allowance period.[3] In each of the first three years of the investment, the investor receives a credit equal to 5% of the total amount paid for the stock or capital interest at the time of purchase. For the final four years, the value of the credit is 6% annually. Investors must retain their interest in a qualified equity investment throughout the seven-year period.

The 111th Congress extended and modified the NMTC program authorization. The American Recovery and Reinvestment Tax Act of 2009, P.L. 111-5, increased the NMTC allocation for 2008 and 2009 to $5 billion from $3.5 billion. Further, the Tax Relief, Unemployment Insurance Reauthorization, and Job Creation Act of 2010 (P.L. 111-312) extended the NMTC authorization through 2011 at $3.5 billion per year.

The 112th Congress may choose to reinstate the NMTC. Both H.R. 2655 and H.R. 3224 would reinstate and extend the NMTC through 2016 with allocation authority of $5 billion and $10 billion, respectively.

PROGRAM COMPONENTS

The process by which the NMTC affects eligible low-income communities involves multiple agents and steps. **Figure 1** illustrates the key agents in the NMTC process.

The multiple steps and agents are designed to ensure that the tax credit achieves its primary goal: encouraging investment in low-income communities. For example, the Treasury Department's CDFI reviews NMTC applicants submitted by CDEs, issues tax credit authority to those CDEs deemed most qualified, and plays a significant role in program compliance.

Community Development Entities (CDE)

A CDE is a domestic corporation or partnership that is an intermediary vehicle for the provision of loans, investment funding, or financial counseling in low-income communities (LICs). To become certified as a CDE, an organization must submit an application to the CDFI that demonstrates that it meets three criteria: (1) it is a domestic corporation or partnership duly organized under the laws of the jurisdiction in which it is incorporated, (2) it has a primary mission of serving low-income communities, and (3) it maintains accountability to residents of these low-income communities. A CDE may demonstrate meeting the third criterion by filling at least 20% of either its advisory or its governing board positions with representatives of low-income communities.[4]

Only CDEs may apply for the NMTC. Upon receipt of NMTC allocation, CDEs attract investors using the credits. While both for-profit and nonprofit CDEs may apply for the NMTC, only for-profit CDEs may pass the NMTC on to investors. To ensure that projects are selected on economic merit, nonprofit CDEs awarded NMTCs must transfer their allocations to for-profit subsidiaries prior to offering NMTCs to investors.

As **Figure 1** illustrates, CDEs play a critical role in a properly functioning NMTC process. CDEs are the intermediaries between the potential low-income community investments and the CDFI during the application process. CDEs also present investors with investment opportunities and provide the CDFI the majority of its compliance data.

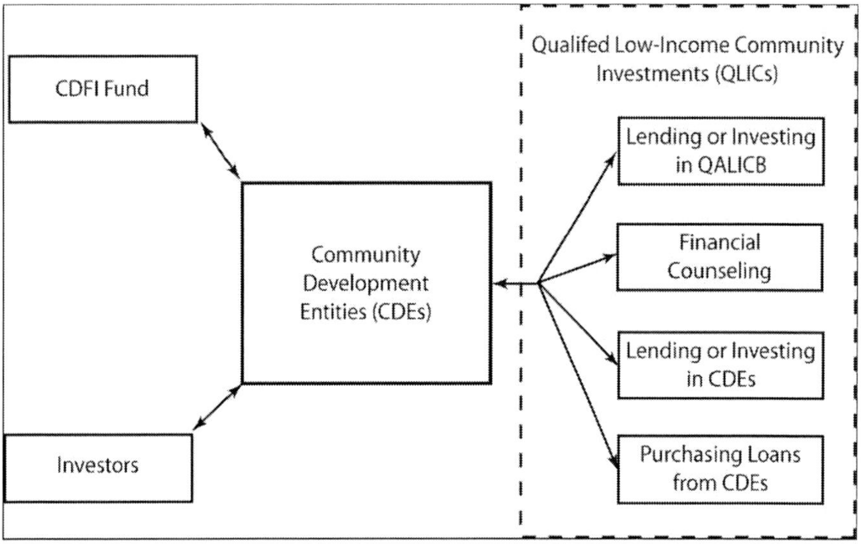

Source: CRS analysis of NMTC program components.

Figure 1. Key Components of the NMTC Process.

Qualifying Low-Income Communities

Under the tax code's NMTC provisions, only eligible investments in qualifying low-income communities are eligible for the NMTC. Qualifying low-income communities include census tracts that have at least one of the following criteria: (1) a poverty rate of at least 20%; (2) is located in a metropolitan area, a median family income below 80% of the greater of the statewide or metropolitan area median family income; or (3) is located outside a metropolitan area, a median family income below 80% of the median statewide family income.

As defined by the criterion above, about 39% of the nation's census tracts covering nearly 36% of the U.S. population are eligible for the NMTC. Additionally, designated targeted populations may be treated as low-income communities.[5]

Further, the definition of a low-income community includes census tracts with low populations and census tracts within high migration rural counties. As a result of the definition of qualified low-income communities, virtually all of the country's census tracts are potentially eligible for the NMTC.

Qualified Investors and Investments

All taxable investors are eligible to receive the NMTC. As noted above, investors receiving the credit can claim the NMTC over a seven-year period, starting on the date of the investment and on each anniversary, at a rate of 5% for each of the first three years and a rate of 6% for each of the next four years, for a total of 39%. Once the investor begins claiming the NMTC, the credit can be recaptured if the CDE (1) ceases to be a CDE, (2) fails to use substantially all of the proceeds for eligible purposes, or (3) redeems the investment principal.[6]

Almost all qualified equity investments (QEI) in low-income communities or serving low-income populations could be eligible to receive the NMTC. These eligible investments are referred to as qualified low-income community investments (QLICIs). QLICIs are categorized in four ways: (1) loans or investments to qualified active low-income community businesses (QALICB), (2) the provision of financial counseling, (3) loans or investments in other CDEs, and (4) the purchase of loans from other CDEs.[7] All QLICIs, including QALICBs, are explicitly prohibited from investing in residential rental property and certain types of businesses, such as golf courses and casinos.

NMTC Allocation Process and Compliance

To receive an allocation, a CDE must submit an application to the CDFI, which asks a series of standardized questions about the track record of the CDE, the amount of NMTC allocation authority being requested, and the CDE's plans for any allocation authority granted.

The application covers four areas: (1) the CDE's business strategy to invest in low-income communities, (2) capitalization strategy to raise equity from investors, (3) management capacity, and (4) expected impact on jobs and economic growth in low-income communities where investments are to be made. In addition, priority points are available for addressing the statutory priorities of investing in unrelated entities and having demonstrated a track record of serving disadvantaged businesses or communities. The application is reviewed and scored to identify those applicants most likely to have the greatest community development impact and ranked in descending order of aggregate score. Tax credit allocations are then awarded based upon the aggregate ranking, until all of the allocation authority is exhausted. In each of the four completed NMTC rounds, significantly more CDEs applied for allocations than were able to receive allocations, with only 22% of applicants receiving allocations. Additionally, allocation authority of $107 billion was requested, compared with the $12.1 billion in allocation authority available.[8] Prior to receiving the authority to offer tax credits to investors, every CDE allocatee must sign an allocation agreement. The allocation agreement clarifies the terms and conditions of the allocation authority, such as the total tax credit authority, service areas, authorized uses of the allocation, and CDE reporting requirements. Failing to meet the terms of the allocation agreement subjects the CDE to the potential revocation of allocation authority. Additionally, the Internal Revenue Service (IRS) monitors compliance with the tax consequences of NMTC allocations, focusing on the "substantially all" requirement. As specified in the IRS regulations, CDE allocatees must issue tax credits to investors within five years of signing their allocation agreements and invest the QEIs in QLICIs within 12 months of signing their allocation agreements. If these requirements are not satisfied, the CDE loses the authority to allocate the unused NMTC. In addition, CDEs that receive principal payments from their QLICIs have 12 months to reinvest those funds in QLICIs to avoid recapture.

NMTC Investment Activity

Once an allocatee signs its allocation agreement and receives its NMTC allocation authority, it may begin soliciting capital from investors. Column 2 of **Table 1** lists the total allocation awarded to date by the NMTC, by funding round. Investors receive the right to claim NMTCs on a portion of their investment, by acquiring stock or a capital interest in a CDE with an allocation. The CDE, in turn, must invest the proceeds in qualified low-income community investments. Investors have, to date, invested roughly $26.1 billion in CDEs. Columns 3 and 4 list the remaining available NMTC allocation, in dollars and as a percentage, that have not yet been allocated to an investor, by round.

Legislative Developments

Modifications to the NMTC program have been made in each Congress since the NMTC was created. In the 108th Congress, the American Jobs

Creation Act of 2004 (P.L. 108-357, 118 Stat. 1418) included provisions expanding the authority of the Secretary of the Treasury to treat certain other tracts and targeted populations as low-income communities.[9]

Table 1. NMTC Qualified Equity Investment, by Allocation Round

Allocation Round (Year)	Total Allocation	Remaining Available Allocation	Percent Remaining
Round 1 (2001-2002)	$2,491,000,000	$526,165.13	0.02%
Round 2 (2003-2004)	$3,500,000,000	$6,055,849.71	0.17%
Round 3 (2005)	$2,000,000,000	$35,170,000.00	1.76%
Round 4 (2006)	$4,100,000,000	$235,000.00	0.01%
Round 5 (2007)	$3,909,000,000	$211,790,871.52	5.42%
Round 6 (2008)	$5,000,000,000	$543,535,499.16	10.87%
Round 7 (2009)	$5,000,000,000	$1,082,681,252.83	21.65%
Round 8 (2010)	$3,500,000,000	$1,485,976,056.17	42.46
Round 9 (2011)	$3,500,000,000	—	—
Total[a, b]	**$29,500,000,000**	**$3,365,970,694.52**	**10.20%**

Source: CRS analysis of NMTC Qualified Equity Investment Report (February 14, 2012).

a. Columns may not sum to total due to rounding.

b. Totals do not include the allocation for 2011 due to their being recently awarded.

During the 109th Congress, the Gulf Opportunity Zone Act of 2005 (P.L. 109-135, 119 Stat. 2577) was enacted to provide tax relief to businesses and individuals affected by Hurricanes Katrina, Wilma, and Rita. The bill, which created the Gulf Opportunity Zone (or GO Zone), provided an additional $1 billion in allocation authority to CDEs with a significant mission in the recovery and redevelopment of low-income communities in the Katrina GO Zone.[10]

Also during the 109th Congress, the Tax Relief and Health Care Act of 2006 (P.L. 109-432, 120 Stat. 2922) extended the NMTC for one year, through 2008, with an additional allocation of $3.5 billion and mandated Treasury to promulgate regulations to ensure that non-metropolitan counties receive a proportional allocation of investments under the NMTC.

In the 110th Congress, legislative attention focused primarily on extending the NMTC program authorization. This attention came to fruition with the enactment of P.L. 110-343, which extended the NMTC program authorization one year, through the end of 2009. This one-year extension was also proposed in H.R. 6049, S. 2886, S. 3098, and H.R. 7060. In addition, H.R. 2075 and S. 1239 proposed to extend the NMTC through 2013 and would have authorized allocations of $3.5 billion, indexed for inflation, for each of the years. Also introduced during the 110th Congress, H.R. 3907 proposed to make the NMTC permanent.

In the 111th Congress, the American Recovery and Reinvestment Tax Act of 2009, P.L. 111-5, which was signed into law on February 17, 2009, increased the NMTC allocation for 2008 and 2009, to $5 billion from $3.5 billion. For the additional 2008 allocation, the CDFI Fund distributes the additional $1.5 billion in NMTCs to applicants of the original 2008 allocation round. Also in the 111th Congress, the Tax Relief, Unemployment Insurance Reauthorization, and Job Creation Act of 2010 (P.L. 111-312) extended the NMTC authorization through 2011 at $3.5 billion per year.

In the 112th Congress H.R. 2655 and H.R. 3224 would both extend the NMTC through 2016 with allocation authority of $5 billion and $10 billion, respectively.

POLICY CONSIDERATIONS

The New Markets Tax Credit Program expired at the end of 2011. As Congress debates reauthorization of the NMTC, the following policy considerations could be pertinent to any consideration of these bills.

The NMTC is primarily intended to encourage private capital investment in eligible low-income communities. However, the source of the investment funds has implications for the effectiveness of the program in achieving its objective. From an economic perspective, the impact of the NMTC would be greatest in the case where the investment represents new investment in the U.S. economy that would not have occurred in the absence of the program. Conversely, the impact of the NMTC is diminished to the extent the tax credit is applied to investment that would have otherwise occurred or been funded by a shift in investment from more productive alternatives.[11]

To date, only one study has empirically assessed the question of whether NMTC investment is funded through shifted investment or whether it represents new investment.[12] The findings of the study suggest that corporate investment represented a shift in investment location. In contrast, the authors concluded that a portion of individual NMTC investment, roughly $641 million, represented new investment.

Although important, understanding the source of NMTC investments alone is not sufficient to determine the effectiveness of the NMTC. A comprehensive review of the program would require an accounting of both the social and economic costs and benefits of the NMTC, an undertaking which may pose considerable challenges. For example, this would include examining the efficiency and opportunity costs of the NMTC investments, while a comprehensive accounting of the NMTC benefits would need to identify and value "spillovers" such as its effect on neighboring businesses and communities. The CDFI Fund is working with a contractor on a comprehensive review of the NMTC, which may include an assessment of the effectiveness of the NMTC.

Others, notably GAO, have recommended that the NMTC be simplified by converting the NMTC into a grant program.[13] This option may be able to deliver the same level of incentive with lower cost to the government, as investors do not generally "buy" tax credits at face value—allowing a smaller grant to provide a similar level of incentive. Specifically, tax credit markets historically set a price of 70 to 80 cents per dollar of tax credit, with lower valuations in recent years due to tight credit markets and decreased corporate profits.

A grant option, however, likely provides a lesser incentive for investors to invest in NMTC projects, as they may not be the beneficiary of the incentive.[14] If this occurs, improving the access to capital in low-income communities (an NMTC program goal) would be more difficult. Further, a grant program may complicate existing mechanisms designed to ensure the NMTC is used for intended purposes, as CDEs are likely less capitalized than investors and the possible removal of IRS authority to recapture benefits (as the NMTC would no longer be a tax program).

An additional issue is the geographic distribution of NMTC activity. Initial concerns focused on distinctions between urban and rural NMTC activity and have been addressed through legislation. Further, NMTC activity has occurred in all 50 states, the District of Columbia, and Puerto Rico. However, the distribution of NMTC activity appears concentrated in a few states—with the nine states with the highest activity accounting for over 50% of all NMTC activity.[15] In contrast, the 25 states with the least NMTC activity account for less than 10% of all NMTC activity. The current distribution of activity is not likely to reflect the distribution of low-income populations and may raise questions concerning the equity of the NMTC.

Finally, the NMTC is one of several programs designed to improve conditions in low-income communities. In a 2004 assessment of the NMTC, the Office of Management and Budget noted that the goal of the NMTC overlaps that of several other tax credits and numerous programs administered by the Departments of Housing and Urban Development and Commerce.[16] Given this overlap and the desire to target federal funds to their most productive uses, it follows that information on the performance of the NMTC relative to other programs with a similar goal would be of use. To date, however, no comparative, empirical study of this nature has been undertaken.

End Notes

[1] Congress provided a schedule limiting the NMTC allocation authority for calendar years 2001 through 2007. The schedule allowed for $1.0 billion in allocation authority in 2001, $1.5 billion in 2002 and 2003, $2.0 billion in 2004 and 2005, and $3.5 billion in 2006 and 2007.

[2] The Gulf Opportunity Zone Act of 2005 (P.L. 109-135) authorized an additional $1 billion of NMTC equity for qualified investments in areas affected by Hurricane Katrina, the Tax Relief and Health Care Act of 2006 (P.L. 109-432) extended the NMTC for an additional year (through 2008) with an additional $3.5 billion of NMTC allocation authority, and the Emergency Economic Stabilization Act of 2008 (P.L. 110-343) extended the NMTC for an additional year (through 2009) with an additional $3.5 billion of NMTC allocation authority. In the 111th Congress, the American Recovery and Reinvestment Tax Act of 2009, P.L. 111-5, increased the NMTC allocation for 2008 and 2009, to $5 billion from $3.5 billion and the Tax Relief, Unemployment Insurance Reauthorization, and Job Creation Act of 2010 (P.L. 111-312) extended the NMTC authorization through 2011 at $3.5 billion per year.

[3] In present value terms, the credit is equal to approximately 30% of the eligible investment at a 6.7% discount rate.

[4] In addition, all Community Development Financial Institutions or Specialized Small Business Investment Companies automatically qualify as CDEs. To be recognized as CDEs, these entities are required to register through the CDFI Fund website.

[5] See Internal Revenue Bulletin 2006-29, Notice 2006-60, issued July 17, 2006, for a more complete description of the definition of designated targeted populations.

[6] According to IRS regulations, the "substantially all" requirement is met if at least 85% of investor proceeds are used to make eligible investments in the first six years of the NMTC period and at least 75% in year seven of the investment.

[7] For a business to be a QALICB, it must be located in a qualifying census tract, derive at least 50% of gross income from activity conducted in a LIC, have at least 40% of both the use of tangible property and services provided located or performed in the LIC, and have less than 5% of the aggregate unadjusted bases of the property attributable to collectibles or non-qualified financial property.

[8] See U.S. Government Accountability Office, *TAX POLICY: New Markets Tax Credit Appears to Increase Investment by Investors in Low-Income Communities, but Opportunities Exist to Better Monitor Compliance*, GAO-07-296, January 31, 2007, for detailed breakdowns of application and allocation statistics.

[9] The term "targeted population," as defined in 12 U.S.C. 4702(20), means individuals, or an identifiable group of individuals, including an Indian tribe, who (1) are low-income persons (low-income targeted population) or (2) otherwise lack adequate access to loans or equity investments.

[10] The Gulf Opportunity Zone (GO ZONE) is defined as those areas in Alabama, Mississippi, and Louisiana that have been designated by the federal government as warranting assistance due to Hurricane Katrina. Disaster areas associated with hurricanes Rita and Wilma are not eligible for the additional allocation.

[11] However, from a policy perspective, the desire to minimize the distortion of investment choice caused by the NMTC is usually balanced against other objectives, such as equity.

[12] Tami Gurley-Calvez et al., "Do tax incentives affect investment? An analysis of the New Markets Tax Credit," *Public Finance Review*, vol. 34, no. 4, pp. 371-398.

[13] U.S. Government Accountability Office, *New Markets Tax Credit: The Credit Helps Fund a Variety of*, GAO-10-334, January 29, 2011, http://www.gao.gov/products/GAO-10-334.

[14] Allowing CDEs to assign the grants to specific investors is an option to mitigate this problem.

[15] These figures are based upon CRS analysis of CDFI Fund data on investments though FY2010. The data are available at http://www.cdfifund.gov/docs/2011/nmtc/NMTC%20Projects%20Through%202010%20REVISED-2.xls.

[16] See U.S. Office of Management and Budget, *Detailed Information on the New Markets Tax Credit Assessment*, updated January 29, 2008, http://www.whitehouse.gov/omb/expectmore/detail/10002230.2004.html.

In: The Community Development …
Editor: Andre L. Wright
ISBN: 978-1-62417-551-0

Chapter 3

Community Development Financial Institutions and New Markets Tax Credit Programs in Metropolitan and Nonmetropolitan Areas*

United States Government Accountability Office

April 26, 2012

The Honorable Richard Durbin
Chairman
The Honorable Jerry Moran
Ranking Member
Subcommittee on Financial Services and General Government
Committee on Appropriations
United States Senate

The Honorable Jo Ann Emerson
Chairman
The Honorable Jose E. Serrano
Ranking Member
Subcommittee on Financial Services and General Government

---

* This is an edited, reformatted and augmented version of the United States Government Accountability Office, GAO-12-547R, dated April 26, 2012.

Committee on Appropriations
House of Representatives

The Riegle Community Development and Regulatory Improvement Act of 1994 created the Community Development Financial Institutions (CDFI) Fund under the Department of the Treasury to help promote access to capital and credit in underserved urban and rural communities across the country.[1] The CDFI Fund carries out this mission through two primary programs: the CDFI Program and the New Markets Tax Credit (NMTC) Program. The CDFI Program awards financial and technical assistance to CDFIs for financial and development services, cash or capital reserves, operating expenses, and capacity building. CDFIs are specialized financial institutions—including community development banks and credit unions and nonregulated institutions such as loan and venture capital funds—that operate in markets underserved by traditional financial institutions. The NMTC Program, created by the Community Renewal Tax Relief Act of 2000, allocates tax credit authority (in this report, tax credits) to community development entities (CDE), which are domestic corporations or partnerships with a primary mission of serving low-income communities or low-income persons that act as intermediaries in providing loans, investments, or financial counseling in low-income communities.[2] CDEs can use the tax credits to attract equity investments from investors who can, in turn, claim a tax credit over 7 years totaling 39 percent of their qualifying equity investment.[3] The CDFI Program awarded a total of $443 million to CDFIs from fiscal years 2004 through 2010, while the NMTC Program allocated tax credits worth $27 billion to CDEs from fiscal years 2003 through 2010.[4] Both programs' statutes include provisions requiring them to ensure at least a minimum level of assistance to nonmetropolitan areas.

House Report 112-136, referenced by the Consolidated Appropriations Act of 2012, requires that we conduct a study on the concentration of CDFIs and NMTCs in urban areas and comment on the extent that program design, administration, or history contributed to the early establishment of CDFIs in urban areas.[5] In this report, we examine (1) how the CDFI Fund awards funds and allocates tax credits to recipients and how program policies affect the amount of funding and tax credits to metropolitan and nonmetropolitan areas, and (2) the extent to which the amounts of program awards and allocations that recipients receive differ in metropolitan and nonmetropolitan areas. We used the terms "metropolitan" and "nonmetropolitan" to make geographic distinctions between areas that have urban and rural characteristics for consistency in presentation and because some of the data available in program reports use these designations.

To address the first objective, we reviewed documentation related to the CDFI Fund's policies and procedures for distributing financial and technical assistance awards and tax credits to certified CDFIs and CDEs, respectively. We also reviewed CDFI Fund documents, laws, and regulations, prior GAO reports, and other applicable documentation to determine how CDFI and NMTC program policies and other factors have affected the amount of funding and tax credits directed to CDFIs and CDEs in metropolitan and nonmetropolitan areas. To address the second objective, we analyzed CDFI Fund data on primary geographic areas (metropolitan or nonmetropolitan) served by CDFIs that received awards or allocations, the total amounts of awards and allocations CDFIs and CDEs received, and amounts of funding and investments they deployed to metropolitan and nonmetropolitan areas. Our review focused on the period for which complete transaction-level data were available for individual transactions from the CDFI Fund's Community Investment Impact System database. Specifically, we examined data from fiscal years 2004 through 2010 for the CDFI Program and fiscal years 2003 through 2010 for the NMTC Program.[6] The transaction-level data for the CDFI Program represent CDFIs' loans and investments outstanding (which we refer to as total portfolio outstanding) at the end of each reporting year and reflect CDFI Program awards combined with all of the CDFIs' other funding sources. In other words, the data do not allow us to identify which loans and investments outstanding, or how much of the dollar amount of CDFIs' total portfolios outstanding, resulted directly from CDFI Program awards. In addition, because not all CDFI awardees must report transaction-level data, we cannot generalize the findings to the entire CDFI awardee (recipient) population. We examined trends in the amount and number of CDFI- and CDE-financed projects in metropolitan and nonmetropolitan areas. We interviewed CDFI Fund officials and reviewed information from the CDFI Fund and its data contractors on the steps taken to ensure the reliability of their data. For example, we reviewed their processes for ensuring consistent data entry and for addressing potentially inaccurate data. We also checked the data for extreme values and missing data points. We determined that the data were reliable for our purposes.

We conducted this performance audit from January to April 2012 in accordance with generally accepted government auditing standards. Those standards require that we plan and perform the audit to obtain sufficient, appropriate evidence to provide a reasonable basis for our findings and conclusions based on our audit objectives. We believe that the evidence obtained provides a reasonable basis for our findings and conclusions based on our audit objectives. Enclosure I provides a more-detailed description of our scope and methodology.

RESULTS IN BRIEF

The policies and procedures of the CDFI and NMTC Programs help ensure that awards and allocations generally are proportionate to the numbers of qualified applicants that serve metropolitan and nonmetropolitan areas. The CDFI Program's authorizing legislation and regulations require that award recipients constitute a geographically diverse group, serving metropolitan and nonmetropolitan areas and Native communities from different U.S. regions. To meet this requirement, CDFI Program officials have used the application review process and established a goal of matching the proportion of awards to the proportion of qualified applicants that primarily serve nonmetropolitan areas. This proportion changed from year to year depending on the number of qualified applicants that served nonmetropolitan areas. According to officials, revisions to the award procedures in the fiscal year 2012 funding round will enhance the CDFI Program's ability to achieve proportionality. In 2006, Congress, in the Tax Relief and Health Care Act of 2006, added a requirement for the NMTC Program that nonmetropolitan counties receive a proportional allocation of qualified equity investments.[7] To meet this requirement, in 2008, the NMTC Program implemented two goals in its application review process. The first goal requires that a proportionate number of tax credits are allocated to recipients that principally serve nonmetropolitan counties.[8] The second goal requires that at least 20 percent of all community investments resulting from the annual NMTC allocations are made in eligible nonmetropolitan counties.

The programs awarded the majority of funds and tax credits to recipients that served metropolitan areas, but both generally met their proportionality goals with regard to ensuring assistance to nonmetropolitan areas. From fiscal years 2004 through 2010, CDFI Program financial assistance awards to recipients serving primarily nonmetropolitan areas were proportional to the number of qualified applicants that served those areas in every year except 2008. For example, in 2010, 29 percent of award recipients primarily served nonmetropolitan areas, exceeding that year's proportionality goal of 27 percent. Based on recipients' annual reporting for fiscal years 2004 through 2010, about 18 percent of recipients' total annual loans and investments outstanding were in nonmetropolitan areas. For the NMTC Program, since implementing the two proportionality goals in the calendar year 2008 round, program officials stated that they have been successful in helping ensure that a proportional number of tax credits went to recipients that serve nonmetropolitan areas and that 20 percent of all NMTC investments were committed to nonmetropolitan areas. From calendar years 2008 through 2011, recipients committed to deploy more than $3 billion, or 20 percent of total investments, in nonmetropolitan areas. In 2010, the proportion of the dollar amount of NMTC projects financed that went to nonmetropolitan areas increased to 21 percent, which exceeded the program goal of 20 percent.

BACKGROUND

In general, financial institutions must be certified as CDFIs or CDEs before they can receive CDFI Program awards or NMTC allocations, respectively. Table 1 lists the criteria that entities must meet to become certified. For example, CDFIs and CDEs generally must be legal entities that provide the majority of their financial services to low-income persons or communities and maintain accountability to those communities by having members that represent them on their governing or advisory boards. The CDFI Fund follows detailed procedures to ensure that certified entities meet the criteria.

As of February 29, 2012, there were a total of 977 certified CDFIs and 5,500 certified CDEs, including subsidiary CDEs.[9] Enclosure II lists the numbers of certified CDFIs and CDEs by state. The total number of certified CDFIs and CDEs is much higher than the number that typically applies for and obtains program awards in any given year. In addition, not all financial institutions that seek certification will obtain it. Certification rates for CDFIs averaged about 77 percent from fiscal years 2004 through 2010, while CDEs obtained certification about 91 percent of the time from calendar years 2003 through 2010 (see table 2). Agency officials told us that, based on their analysis of fiscal year 2011 certification data, the most common reasons for denying CDFI certification applications were failure to meet the criteria for primary service to eligible target markets and accountability to those markets. They stated that in prior years, these were also two of the most common reasons for denials of certification applications. Failure to meet the financing entity criteria was also historically a reason for denial. They attributed the majority of CDE certification denials to failure to establish accountability to low-income communities.

Table 1. Eligibility Criteria for CDFI and CDE Certification

CDFI	CDE
• Be a legal entity • Have a primary mission of promoting community development • Primarily provide financial products, development services, or other similar financing in arms-length transactions • Primarily serve (direct at least 60 percent of financial product activities to) one or more geographic investment areas meeting certain poverty or income standards; low-income targeted populations; or other targeted populations that lack adequate access to capital and historically have been denied credit • Provide development services—such as credit or homebuyer counseling—in conjunction with financial products • Maintain accountability to defined target markets through representation on governing or advisory board or through outreach activities • Be a nongovernment entity and not be under control of any government entity (except tribal governments)	• Be a legal entity and a domestic corporation or partnership for federal tax purposes • Have a primary mission of serving or providing investment capital to low-income communities or low-income persons and target at least 60 percent of activities to these groups • Maintain accountability to low-income communities through representation on governing or advisory board • Note: Certified CDFIs and Specialized Small Business Investment Companies automatically qualify as CDEs and only need to register as CDEs rather than apply for certification.

Sources: CDFI Fund; CDFI and NMTC Program statutes and regulations.

Table 2. Certification Rates for CDFIs (Fiscal Years 2004-2010) and CDEs (Calendar Years 2003-2010)

	2003	2004	2005	2006	2007	2008	2009	2010	Total
CDFIs									
Certified	N/A	34	72	144	32	32	71	162	**547**
Declined	N/A	50	15	11	12	15	32	30	**165**
Certification rate	N/A	40%	83%	93%	73%	68%	69%	84%	**77%**
CDEs									
Certified	211	153	155	33	121	100	104	134	**1,011**
Declined	18	14	12	3	9	9	16	21	**102**
Certification rate	92%	92%	93%	92%	93%	92%	87%	86%	**91%**

Source: GAO analysis of CDFI Fund data.

Note: The CDE certification rates in this table include only "applicant CDEs" and exclude subsidiary CDEs.

The CDFI Program provides financial or technical assistance to CDFIs to enhance their ability to make loans and investments and provide services for the benefit of designated investment areas, targeted populations, or both.[10] CDFIs can apply for (1) financial assistance awards, which can be used for financial products or services such as loans and checking and savings accounts, development services such as financial or homeownership counseling, loan loss and capital reserves, and operations; or (2) technical assistance awards, which can be used for capacity-building purposes such as personnel salary, professional services, travel, training, and equipment and supplies. As shown in table 3, financial assistance applicants may apply as regular applicants or as Small and Emerging CDFI Assistance (SECA) applicants. SECA applicants are CDFIs that have smaller assets or have been operating for fewer than 5 years. However, regular applicants can apply for more financial assistance funding (for the fiscal year 2011 funding round, up to $2 million) than SECA applicants (which can apply for $600,000). Technical assistance awards were capped in fiscal year 2011 at $100,000 per awardee. Since 1994, the CDFI Program has disbursed more than $1 billion in financial and technical assistance awards.

Congress created the NMTC Program in 2000 under the CDFI Fund to encourage investors to make investments in impoverished, low-income communities that traditionally lack access to capital. CDEs may apply for and receive tax credits, at which point investors can make qualified equity investments by acquiring stock or a capital interest in the CDEs in exchange for the ability to claim the tax credits on a portion of their investment. The CDEs, in turn, must use at least 85 percent of the investment proceeds for community investments, which can be in qualified low-income community businesses and used for residential, commercial, and industrial projects or can be used for other types of activities, such as purchasing loans from other CDEs.[11] Since its inception, the NMTC Program has awarded $33 billion in tax credits to CDEs. The program expired at the end of 2011, but legislation has been proposed to extend it and the administration has asked for an extension in its 2013 budget proposal.[12]

The CDFI and NMTC Programs use varying terminology to describe program activity geographically, depending on the program stage. For example, in the application stage, both programs ask applicants to indicate whether they primarily serve major urban, minor urban, or rural (nonmetropolitan for the NMTC Program) areas.[13] The programs also require awardees and allocatees to commit to the areas that they will serve with their awards and tax credits. At this point, the terminologies diverge. While the

CDFI Program continues to use the major and minor urban and rural classifications, the NMTC Program uses the metropolitan and nonmetropolitan classifications as defined by the 1999 Office of Management and Budget bulletin, with the former term referring to a metropolitan statistical area with a core city or urban center of population 50,000 or more and its surrounding communities and the latter term referring to anything other than a metropolitan area.[14] Finally, when agency officials collect annual data from awardees and allocatees on the use of their funds, both the CDFI Program data and the NMTC Program data are classified using the 1999 Office of Management and Budget bulletin (the "metropolitan" and "nonmetropolitan" system). To simplify the discussion, this report generally uses metropolitan and nonmetropolitan for both programs, as defined by the Office of Management and Budget.[15] As of 2011, approximately 16 percent of the U.S. population resided in nonmetropolitan areas.[16]

Program Policies and Procedures Aim to Make Awards and Allocations Proportionate to Numbers of Applicants That Serve Nonmetropolitan Areas

CDFI Program

The CDFI Program's policies and procedures for reviewing funding applications and making financial and technical assistance awards are intended to encourage assistance to nonmetropolitan areas. After CDFI Program staff checks all applications for completeness and applicant eligibility, reviewers from outside of the CDFI Fund (three reviewers per financial assistance application and one reviewer per technical assistance application) evaluate the applications.

Specifically, financial and technical assistance applicants are scored on and can receive up to 100 points from each reviewer for criteria such as how they meet the needs of their target market and their delivery capacity. As shown in figure 1, applicants that meet or exceed an overall scoring threshold and a threshold in each of the application sections advance to the second phase of the application review process in which CDFI Program officials determine—based on a final ranking score—which applicants will receive awards and how much they will receive.

Table 3. CDFI Financial and Technical Assistance Program Details

Funding and applicant type		Applicant criteria	Eligible uses for funds	Fiscal year 2011 award cap	Matching fund requirement[a]
Financial Assistance	Regular	Certified or certifiable CDFI[b]	• Financial products • Financial services • Development services • Loan loss reserves • Capital reserves • Operations	$2,000,000	100% match from nonfederal sources
	Small and Emerging CDFI Assistance (SECA)	• Certified or certifiable CDFI • Total assets of up to $5 million (up to $250 million for community development banks and up to $10 million for insured credit unions and venture capital funds) or in operation for fewer than 5 years		$600,000	100% match from nonfederal sources
Technical assistance		Certified, certifiable or emerging CDFI[c]	• Personnel (salary and fringe benefits) • Professional services • Travel • Training • Equipment • Materials/supplies • Other	$100,000	None

Source: CDFI Fund 2011 Notice of Funding Availability, 76 *Fed. Reg.* 68,831.

Notes:

[a] Matching funds must be comparable in form and value to the financial assistance award. Congress waived the matching funds requirement in the fiscal year 2009, 2010, and 2011 federal budgets.

[b] A certifiable CDFI has submitted an application to the CDFI Fund demonstrating that it meets the certification requirements, but the CDFI Fund has not yet officially certified the entity.

[c] An emerging CDFI is an entity that demonstrates to the CDFI Fund that it has an acceptable plan to become a certified CDFI within approximately 3 years.

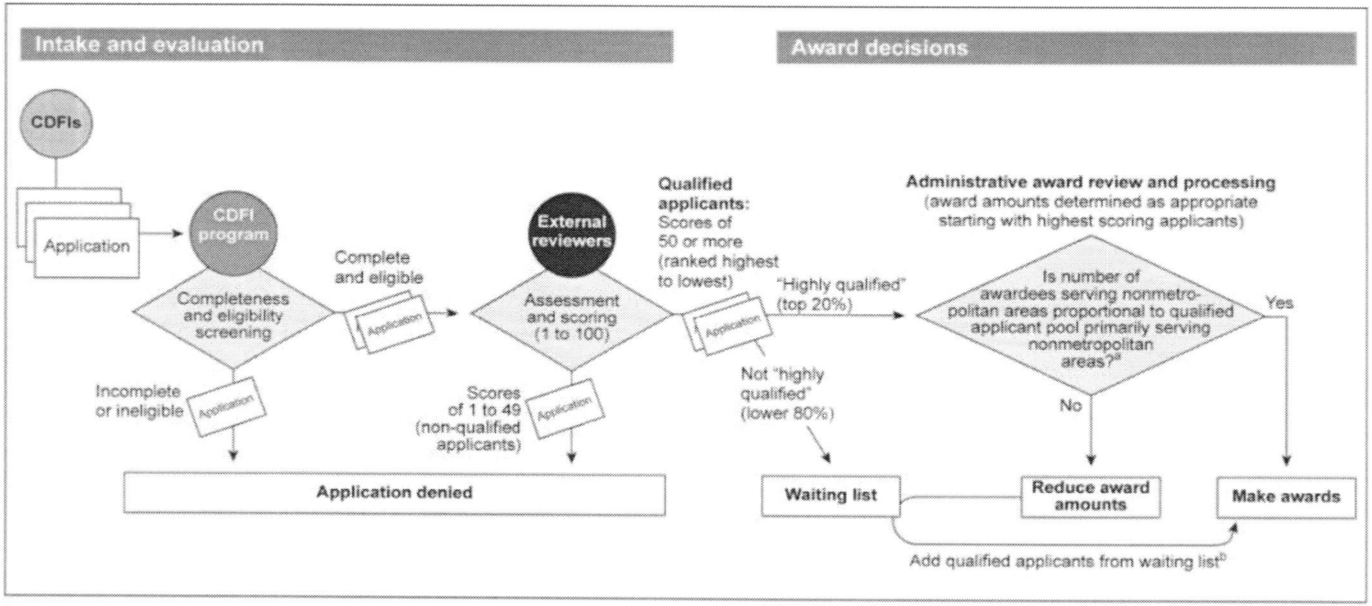

Source: GAO analysis of CDFI Fund data.

[a] CDFI Program officials also check for diversity with regard to geographic region and institution type.

[b] Until the fiscal year 2012 funding round, this process might not have resulted in full proportionality with regard to nonmetropolitan areas. Because reducing award amounts to allow for additional awards could decrease the awards' significance to CDFIs, CDFI Program officials must consider whether award reductions to achieve proportionality are in the best interest of the overall awardee pool.

Figure 1. CDFI Program Financial and Technical Assistance Award Process.

The CDFI Program's authorizing legislation and regulations require that awardees represent a geographically diverse group, serving metropolitan and nonmetropolitan areas and Native communities.[17] According to CDFI Program officials, to meet this requirement, they have tried to match the proportion of awards to the proportion of the qualified applicant pool with nonmetropolitan service areas during the application review process. For example, if 25 percent of qualified applicants in a given funding round indicated a nonmetropolitan service area, the CDFI Program would strive to make 25 percent of the total aggregate number of financial and technical assistance awards to CDFIs with nonmetropolitan service areas. This proportion can change from year to year depending on the number of applicants that serve nonmetropolitan areas and meet the minimum scoring threshold. Until recently, the CDFI Program's procedures did not allow officials to bypass other qualified applicants to select those with nonmetropolitan service areas, which impeded the program's ability to meet desired proportionality goals in certain years. However, for the fiscal year 2012 funding round, the CDFI Program's procedures have been revised to better support goal achievement. That is, CDFI Program officials can now bypass certain applicants on the ordered ranking list to select qualified but lower-ranked applicants to achieve geographic and institutional diversity.

In addition, according to CDFI Program officials, the SECA category for financial assistance awards, as well as the technical assistance awards, is helpful to CDFIs located in or serving nonmetropolitan areas. Officials stated that CDFIs in nonmetropolitan communities are often smaller in asset size and typically have fewer employees than their counterparts in metropolitan communities. The SECA category for financial assistance funding allows CDFIs with assets of less than a certain amount or in operation for fewer than 5 years to apply and compete separately from larger and more established CDFIs. In addition, program officials noted that technical assistance funding is useful to smaller and less established organizations because it can help them build capacity. Technical assistance awards can be used for such items as staff salaries and benefits, consultants, professional services, and computer equipment.[18]

NMTC Program

The NMTC Program's process for making NMTC awards reflects a recent policy change that ensures investment commitments in nonmetropolitan areas. In 2006, Congress required the NMTC Program to ensure that nonmetropolitan counties receive a proportional allocation of qualified equity investments.[19] To guide its implementation of the requirement, in 2007, the CDFI Fund published a Request for Public Comments to obtain feedback on how to define, measure, and ensure "proportionality." Based on the public comments received, NMTC Program officials developed two goals, which they implemented in the calendar year 2008 funding round, to ensure compliance with the new requirement. First, program officials must review the annual allocation decisions and add additional allocatees if necessary to ensure that a proportionate number of applicants that are "rural CDEs"—CDEs that principally serve nonmetropolitan counties—receive tax credits. Second, program officials attempt to ensure through consideration of applicants' commitments to invest in nonmetropolitan areas that at least 20 percent of the aggregate investments made with each round of NMTC allocations are made in eligible nonmetropolitan counties. With regard to the second goal, although public commentators suggested a variety of benchmarks for the minimum proportion to be committed to nonmetropolitan areas, program officials chose 20 percent because it approximated the percentage of the U.S. population that—according to the CDFI Fund's analysis—resided in nonmetropolitan counties.[20] Thus, in recent years, NMTC Program officials have used the review process to ensure proportionate selection on two levels—in terms of areas served and amount of investment committed in those areas.

For the current review process, the NMTC Program first selects a group of three external reviewers with demonstrated experience in business, real estate, or community development finance. Applications are scored on a scale of 100 points for sections on business strategy, community impact, management capacity, and capitalization strategy. Applicants also can receive up to 10 "priority" points by demonstrating a record of successful investment in disadvantaged communities or businesses and by investing in businesses unrelated to the applicant.[21]

CDEs that meet or exceed an overall scoring threshold and a threshold in each of the four application sections listed previously advance to the second phase of the review, in which a panel of up to three NMTC Program officials determine—based on a final ranking score—which CDEs will receive allocations and how much they will receive. NMTC Program staff review the amount of tax credits that the CDEs requested and, based on the information in the application materials, award preliminary allocation amounts in the order of CDEs' final ranking scores until the allocations are exhausted. Not all of the CDEs that satisfy the minimum application score thresholds receive allocations.[22]

After making award decisions, the NMTC Program analyzes the allocatee pool to determine whether it has met the two proportionality goals. If the percentage of allocatees that are rural CDEs is not at least equal to the percentage of qualified applicants that are rural CDEs, the fund provides allocations to additional qualified rural CDEs from that pool in descending order of their final ranking score until it achieves the appropriate percentage balance. If necessary to accommodate the additional allocatees without exceeding the available tax credits, NMTC Program officials apply a reduction to all allocations to CDEs that have not committed to make at least 20 percent of their community investments in nonmetropolitan areas. For the second proportionality goal, all applicants must specify a minimum and maximum percentage of their community investments that they are willing to commit to nonmetropolitan areas. For example, an applicant might indicate that it will commit to making at least 15 percent but no more than 30 percent of its community investments in nonmetropolitan areas, while another applicant might indicate that it will make all of its community investments in metropolitan areas. NMTC Program officials calculate the minimum amount of community investments that all allocatees have committed to nonmetropolitan areas.

If allocatees have not committed to making at least 20 percent of their aggregate community investments in nonmetropolitan areas, the NMTC Program can require allocatees to direct more investments—up to the maximum percentages they indicated in their applications—to nonmetropolitan areas. If, after applying the maximum percentages, the aggregate commitment to nonmetropolitan areas still does not equal at least 20 percent, the NMTC Program can award additional allocations to rural CDEs in descending order of their final ranking score, applying a formula reduction to all allocations for which allocatees have not committed at least 20 percent of investments to nonmetropolitan areas. Figure 2 illustrates the NMTC allocation process with a hypothetical example.

To address potential challenges in implementing NMTC projects in nonmetropolitan communities, the NMTC Program gives rural CDEs an extra year to raise qualified equity investments and deploy the proceeds for community investments.

Specifically, most CDEs must raise at least 20 percent of their qualified equity investments (in exchange for the tax credits that they can provide to investors) within 1 year after they receive their allocations, and they must deploy the proceeds of those qualified equity investments to qualified businesses within 1 year after raising the investments.

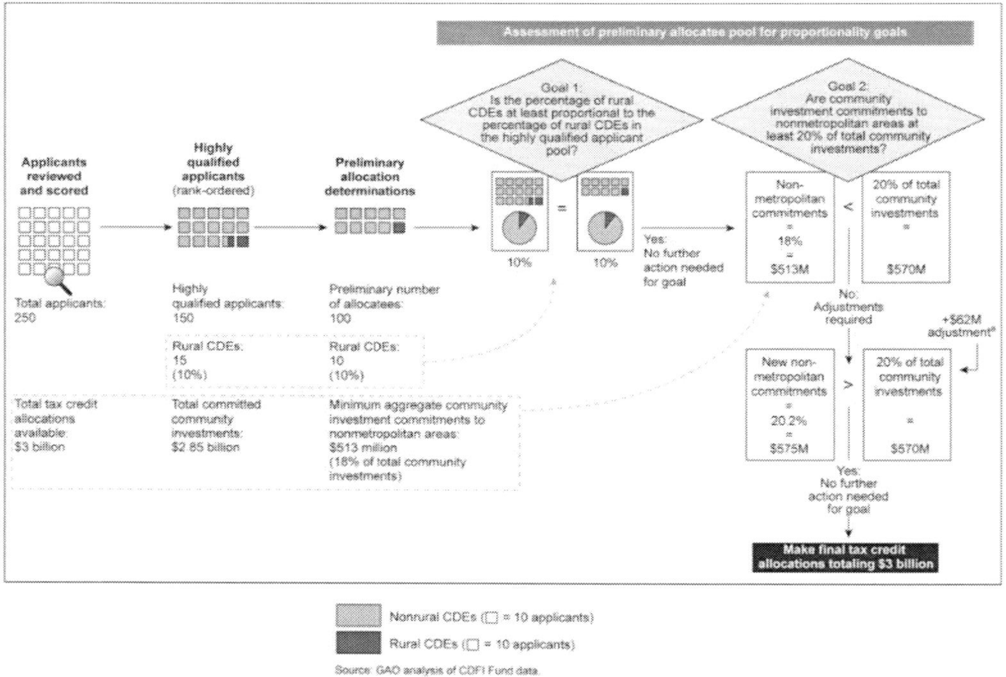

Notes: This figure is an example of applying NMTC Program proportionality goals to hypothetical application information.

[a] Require any or all allocatees to direct additional community investments to nonmetropolitan areas (up to the maximum percentage they committed to in their applications). Based on track records and ability to deploy investments in nonmetropolitan areas, require eight allocatees to direct an additional $62 million in community investments to nonmetropolitan areas.

Figure 2. Illustration of the NMTC Program Allocation Process.

However, rural CDEs receive an extra year to meet these requirements because of the potential difficulties in carrying out NMTC projects in nonmetropolitan areas. In particular, we have previously reported that CDEs can face challenges in using NMTCs to invest in smaller projects because transaction costs, such as legal fees or compliance monitoring costs, tend to be fixed (thus, smaller transactions would not incur lower transaction costs relative to the size of the project).[23] Because of high transaction costs, NMTC Program officials said that the minimum investment size of an NMTC transaction is commonly $5 million to $6 million. They explained that the federal tax structure related to the NMTC Program tends to benefit larger-size projects or deals. This structure may put CDEs that wish to invest in nonmetropolitan areas—where projects can be smaller than in metropolitan areas—at a disadvantage.[24]

Both Programs Directed Most Awards and Tax Credits to Metropolitan Areas, but Generally Met Proportionality Goals for Nonmetropolitan Areas

The CDFI and NMTC Programs awarded the majority of funds and tax credits to recipients that served metropolitan areas, but both generally met their goals with regard to proportionality in nonmetropolitan areas. For both programs, we looked at the differences in the level of assistance provided to metropolitan and nonmetropolitan areas. Specifically, for each of the programs, we looked at the metropolitan and nonmetropolitan distributions of (1) awards and commitments, and (2) total portfolio outstanding (CDFI Program) and projects financed (NMTC Program).

CDFI Program

CDFI Program officials stated that they typically had been able to meet their goal of making awards proportionate to the number of qualified applicants that primarily serve nonmetropolitan areas. We analyzed the financial assistance award data for fiscal years 2004 through 2010 to determine the extent to which the CDFI Program met the geographic diversity goal. During this period, the proportion of awardees that primarily served nonmetropolitan areas equaled or exceeded the proportion of qualified applicants that served these areas every year except in 2008, when awardees serving nonmetropolitan areas represented 26 percent of all awardees compared with 35 percent of all qualified applicants (see table 4).

The total financial and technical assistance award amounts varied for CDFIs primarily serving nonmetropolitan areas.[25] From fiscal years 2004 through 2010, awards to CDFIs that indicated they primarily served nonmetropolitan areas totaled about $126 million, or about 29 percent of the $436 million in all awards for that period, compared with about $311 million (71 percent) that went to CDFIs serving primarily metropolitan areas.[26] As shown in figure 3, the proportion of awards to these CDFIs varied considerably over the review period. However, it averaged just under 30 percent across that time period.

For fiscal years 2004 through 2010, CDFIs' total loans and investments outstanding in nonmetropolitan areas annually averaged about 18 percent of their total portfolios outstanding, reflecting an increase to nonmetropolitan areas in recent years (see figure 4). As stated earlier, CDFIs must report all of their loans and investments outstanding, which includes program awards combined with all of their other sources of funding.[27] From a low of about $55 million in 2004, the dollar amount of CDFIs' total loans and investments outstanding in nonmetropolitan areas grew fivefold in 2005 and then increased steadily until 2009 and marginally decreased in 2010. From 2008 through 2010, CDFIs' total loans and investments outstanding in nonmetropolitan areas exceeded $1 billion annually. As a percentage of CDFIs' total portfolios, the dollar amounts to nonmetropolitan areas remained fairly stable throughout this period. A similar trend occurred in metropolitan areas for the same period, as the total loans and investments outstanding increased fivefold from 2004 to 2005, steadily increased for 3 years, and plateaued at approximately $4.3 billion annually from 2008 through 2010. CDFI Fund officials stated that the growth in both metropolitan and nonmetropolitan total loans and investments outstanding was a result of two factors. First, the overall level of CDFI Program awards increased substantially over the time period. In 2004, total financial and technical assistance awards were about $46 million, and in 2010 the combined awards totaled almost $105 million. Second, partly because of the increase in total awards, the size of the individual CDFIs' assets increased, as reflected by the number and amount of loans and investments made by reporting CDFIs. For example, the total portfolio outstanding for both metropolitan and nonmetropolitan CDFIs in 2004 was $330 million, and the total portfolio outstanding in 2010 was over $5 billion. See enclosure III for more details on CDFIs' loans and investments outstanding in nonmetropolitan areas, by state.

Figure 4 also shows the number of loans and investments that CDFIs made in metropolitan and nonmetropolitan areas from fiscal years 2004 through 2010. CDFIs made more than 290,000 loans and investments in metropolitan areas (73 percent) and more than 109,000 loans and investments in nonmetropolitan areas (27 percent) over the entire period.

Table 4. Proportion of Qualified Applicants and Awardees Serving Nonmetropolitan Areas for CDFI Program, Fiscal Years 2004-2010

Fiscal year	Qualified applicants			Awardees		
	Total	Number serving nonmetropolitan areas	Percentage serving nonmetropolitan areas	Total	Number serving nonmetropolitan areas	Percentage serving nonmetropolitan areas
2004[a]	**78**	21	27%	**67**	19	28%
2005	**124**	37	30%	**48**	17	35%
2006	**121**	28	23%	**52**	15	29%
2007	**119**	26	22%	**49**	11	22%
2008	**158**	56	35%	**66**	17	26%
2009	**337**	89	26%	**121**	33	27%
2010	**292**	79	27%	**147**	42	29%

Source: GAO analysis of CDFI Fund data.

Notes: The data in the table reflect the CDFI Program's financial assistance awards only. Data on technical assistance awards were not readily available within the time frames of this review. According to an official, recipients of technical assistance awards are more likely to serve nonmetropolitan areas. As a result, the percentages in the table are likely understated, but the extent of this difference is limited since the CDFI Program makes considerably fewer technical assistance awards compared with financial assistance awards.

[a] The CDFI Program utilized a different scoring method for regular and Small and Emerging CDFI Assistance (SECA) applicants and a different applicant grouping process to categorize the two applicant types in fiscal year 2004. However, because applicants in 2004 still had to meet a minimum scoring threshold to be considered qualified, we believe that this does not significantly impact our analysis.

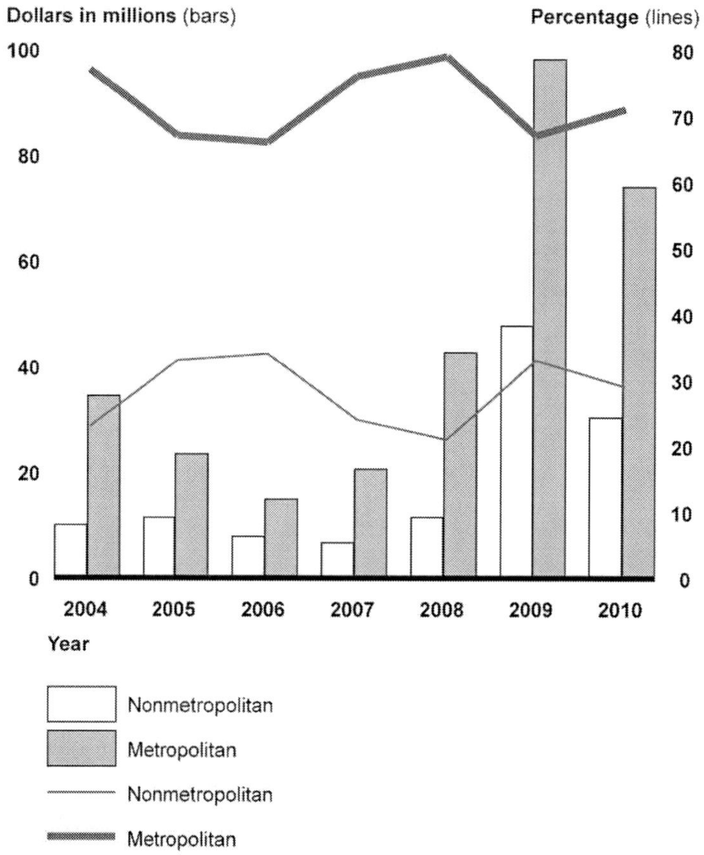

Source: GAO analysis of CDFI Fund data.

Note: The increase in funding amount in the last 2 years of the period is a result of additional funding from the American Recovery and Reinvestment Act in 2009 and a higher appropriation in 2010 than in previous years.

Figure 3. Total Financial and Technical Assistance Award Amounts by CDFIs' Primary Service Area, Fiscal Years 2004-2010.

In addition, the proportion of loans and investments (27 percent) was greater than the proportion dollar amounts (18 percent) of those loans and investments in nonmetropolitan areas for the same period. The percentage of loans and investments in nonmetropolitan areas steadily decreased from its peak at 34 percent in 2006 to 23 percent in 2009.

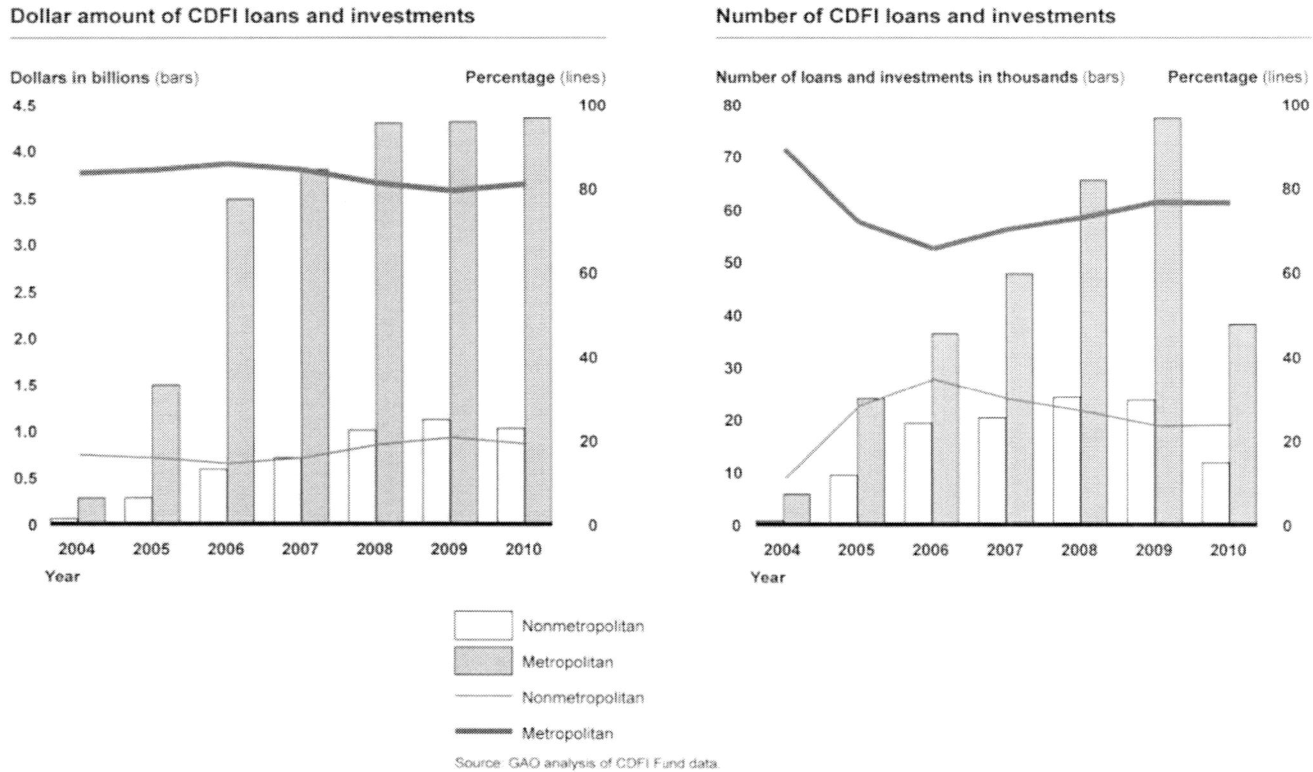

Figure 4. Total Dollar Amount and Number of CDFI Loans and Investments Outstanding in Metropolitan and Nonmetropolitan Areas, Fiscal Years 2004-2010.

NMTC Program

Policy changes to the NMTC Program have helped to ensure that about 20 percent of CDEs' community investments were committed to nonmetropolitan areas in recent years.

Since the two goals related to the proportionality requirement were implemented in the 2008 funding round, the NMTC Program has met the proportionality requirement. For the first proportionality goal, NMTC Program officials stated that they have been able to ensure that a proportional number of rural CDEs received tax credits and, for the second proportionality goal, that 20 percent of all NMTC community investments were committed to nonmetropolitan counties.

From calendar years 2008 through 2011, rural CDEs received tax credits totaling almost $2 billion. On the basis of their designation as rural CDEs, they were obligated to deploy at least 50 percent of this amount in nonmetropolitan areas.

During the same time period, CDEs (including both rural and nonrural CDEs) committed to deploy more than $3 billion, or 20 percent of total investments, in nonmetropolitan areas (see table 5). Data on investment commitments by areas served are not available prior to 2008 because the NMTC Program did not track this information.

Based on our review of annual data reported by CDEs through the fiscal year 2010 reporting period, the proportion of NMTC projects financed in nonmetropolitan areas varied from 2003 through 2010 but increased appreciably in 2010 following the 2008 policy change requiring proportional investments in these areas (see figure 5).[28] From 2003 to 2005, the dollar amount of projects financed in nonmetropolitan areas increased from about $9 million to $239 million (or from 11 percent of total projects financed to 16 percent of total projects financed).

During 2006 to 2009, the dollar amount of projects financed in nonmetropolitan areas fluctuated between a low of $108 million to a high of $401 million. In the last year of the review period, the dollar amount of projects financed in nonmetropolitan areas increased to over $1 billion (or 21 percent of the total amount of projects financed).

The dollar amount of projects financed in metropolitan areas also varied throughout the review period but totaled over $4 billion in both fiscal years 2009 and 2010. See enclosure IV for more details on CDEs' projects financed in nonmetropolitan areas, by state.

Table 5. Total CDE Community Investment Commitments to Nonmetropolitan Counties, Calendar Years 2008-2011

Dollars in millions				
Calendar year	**Total community investments**	**Number of CDEs making nonmetropolitan commitments[a]**	**Total investments committed to nonmetropolitan counties**	**Percentage of total investments committed to nonmetropolitan counties**
2008[b]	$4,895	60	$989	20%
2009	$4,880	49	$971	20%
2010	$3,409	46	$682	20%
2011[c]	$3,526	34	$708	20%
Totals	**$16,710**	**189**	**$3,350**	**20%**

Source: GAO analysis of CDFI Fund data.

[a] The numbers in this column reflect only CDEs that committed to make a minimal percentage of their investments in nonmetropolitan counties, including rural CDEs. CDEs do not have to commit to investments in nonmetropolitan counties. However, if CDEs do so, they must uphold the commitments.

[b] There were two NMTC allocation rounds for applicants that applied in 2008: the regular NMTC annual allocation round and an additional allocation round authorized by the American Recovery and Reinvestment Act. Data in the 2008 row reflect both allocation rounds.

[c] The NMTC Program announced the results of the calendar year 2011 allocation round in February 2012 and provided publicly available data on tax credits to rural CDEs and overall investment commitments to nonmetropolitan counties.

According to an NMTC Program official, for several reasons, NMTC Program data do not immediately reflect the increased investments in nonmetropolitan areas that would be expected to follow from the proportionality goals instituted in 2008. First, some of the 2008 awards were not closed until 2009 under the American Recovery and Reinvestment Act of 2009. Second, rural CDEs have an additional year to raise qualified equity investments and deploy the proceeds as community investments. Lastly, CDEs have up to 180 days after the end of their fiscal year to report to the CDFI Fund on projects financed. Consequently, in 2010, the data for projects financed in nonmetropolitan areas reflect a substantial increase following from the 2008 policy change.

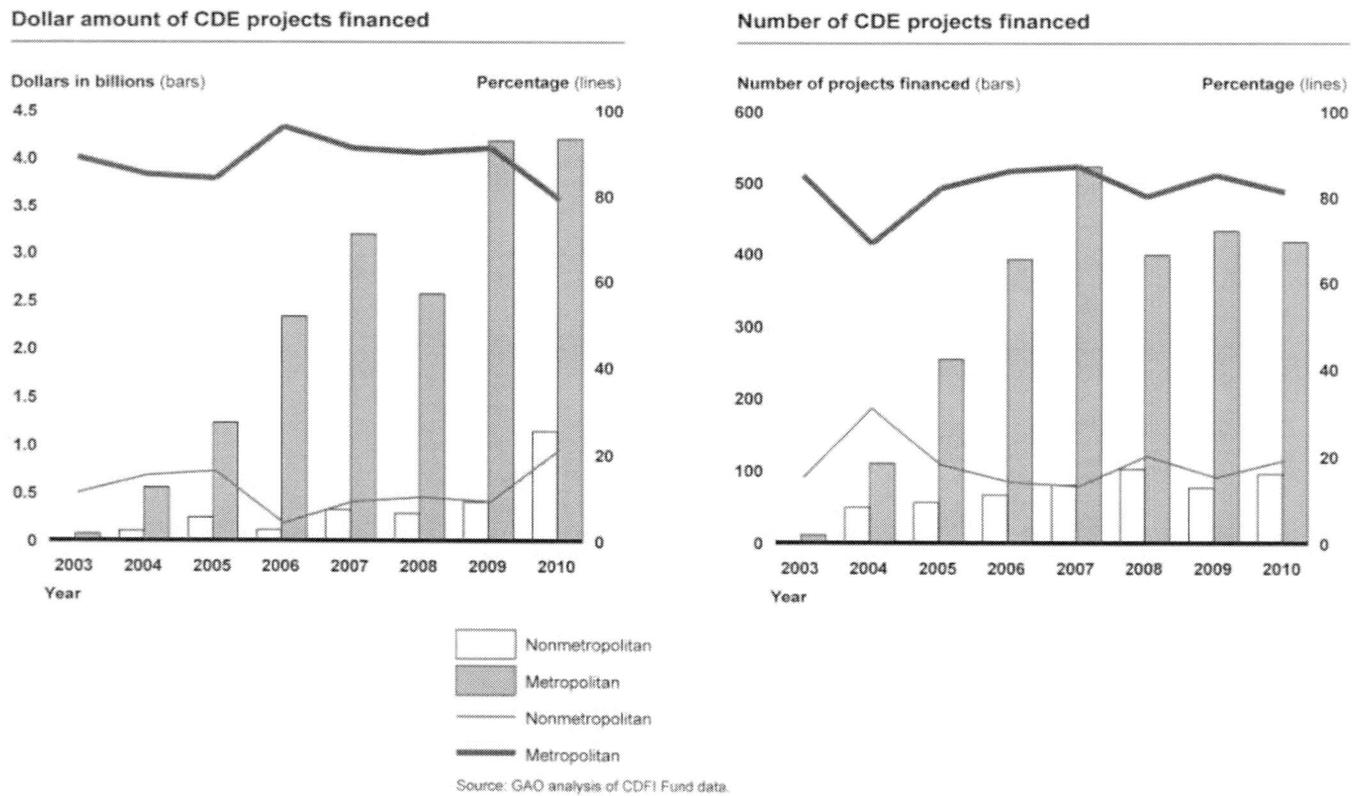

Figure 5. Dollar Amount and Number of CDE Projects Financed in Metropolitan and Nonmetropolitan Areas, Fiscal Years 2003-2010.

AGENCY COMMENTS AND OUR EVALUATION

We provided a draft of this report to the Secretary of the Treasury for review and comment. In its written comments, Treasury concurred with the report's observations regarding the process and distribution of assistance to metropolitan and nonmetropolitan areas for both programs. Treasury also provided technical comments that we incorporated into the report, as appropriate.

Daniel Garcia-Diaz
Acting Director, Financial Markets and Community Investment

ENCLOSURE I. OBJECTIVES, SCOPE, AND METHODOLOGY

The objectives of this report were to assess (1) how the Community Development Financial Institutions (CDFI) Fund awards funds and allocates tax credits to recipients and how program policies affect the amount of funding and tax credits to metropolitan and nonmetropolitan areas, and (2) the extent to which the amounts of program awards and allocations that recipients receive differ in metropolitan and nonmetropolitan areas.

To address the first objective, we reviewed the CDFI and New Markets Tax Credit (NMTC) Programs' policies and procedures for distributing financial and technical assistance awards and tax credits to certified CDFIs and community development entities (CDE), respectively. We reviewed how the programs' policies and procedures considered and weighed applicants' geographic location in making funding and tax credit allocation decisions. We also reviewed annual notices of funding and allocation availability, reports on annual awards and allocations, applicable laws and regulations, prior GAO reports, and other documentation. We further reviewed the CDFI Fund's guidance for certifying CDFIs and CDEs because financial institutions generally must apply to the CDFI Fund for certification as CDFIs or CDEs before they can apply for CDFI awards or NMTC allocations, respectively. We also obtained program data to determine the numbers of approved and denied applicants for CDFI and CDE certification. The CDFI certification data covered fiscal years 2004 through 2010 and the CDE certification data covered calendar years 2003 through 2010. We reviewed lists of all certified CDFIs and CDEs as of February 29, 2012, from the CDFI Fund's website. We also interviewed CDFI Fund officials.

Both programs used varying terms to describe geographic areas such as urban and rural areas. To simplify presentation of geographic designations and develop consistent terminology for use in our report, we consulted with agency officials and agreed to report information using "metropolitan" and "nonmetropolitan" categories. Specifically, the CDFI and NMTC Program applications require applicants to indicate the types of geographic areas they primarily serve—major urban, minor urban, or rural.[29] For CDFI and NMTC Program applicants and awardees that indicated they served primarily major or minor urban areas, we reclassified them as serving metropolitan areas. For applicants and awardees that indicated they served primarily rural areas, we reclassified them as serving nonmetropolitan areas. The transaction-level data we received on CDFIs' loans and investments outstanding and CDEs' projects financed already were presented in metropolitan and nonmetropolitan terms and therefore did not require reclassification.

To address the second objective, we compared program data for metropolitan and nonmetropolitan areas on (1) the number of CDFIs that received awards by primary geographic service area, (2) the total amounts of awards and allocations CDFIs and CDEs received, and (3) the total amounts of funding and investments deployed. We reviewed CDFI and NMTC Program documentation to better understand each program's proportionality goal. We conducted interviews with program officials, including the CDFI Fund Office for Financial Strategies and Research and Office of Certification, Compliance Monitoring and Evaluation to discuss the data captured by the various databases.

Analysis of CDFI Program Awards

The CDFI Program regulations require that awardees represent a geographically diverse group serving metropolitan and nonmetropolitan areas. To assess the CDFI Program's progress toward its geographic diversity goal, we analyzed the proportion of qualified applicants to the proportion of CDFI awardees serving nonmetropolitan areas for fiscal years 2004 through 2010. From the CDFI Program, we obtained financial assistance application and award data on the total number of qualified applicants and awardees.

We calculated the percentage of qualified applicants and awardees serving nonmetropolitan areas. We used financial assistance award data and not technical assistance award data in our analysis of the geographic diversity goal because of time constraints to collect the qualified applicant data broken down by primary areas served. Our analysis of overall award data indicated that recipients of technical assistance awards are slightly more likely to serve nonmetropolitan areas. As a result, our discussion of proportionality in the CDFI Program may understate the percentage of awards that went to CDFIs serving nonmetropolitan areas. However, the extent of this difference is limited since the CDFI Program makes fewer technical assistance awards than financial assistance awards. CDFI Program officials told us that in fiscal year 2004, they used a different scoring method and a different applicant grouping process to categorize regular and Small and Emerging CDFI Assistance (SECA) applicants.[30] We note these differences in our presentation of the 2004 data on proportions of qualified CDFI Program applicants and awardees serving nonmetropolitan areas.

To assess the primary geographic areas that CDFIs reported they served, we analyzed CDFI Program data on award amounts for financial and technical assistance by CDFIs' reported primary geographic market served (metropolitan and nonmetropolitan). We obtained historical application and award data from the CDFI Fund on awardee, primary geographic market, amount of technical assistance funding, and amount of financial assistance funding for fiscal years 2004 through 2010. The applications for financial and technical assistance capture the primary geographic market variable. Applicants can serve a combination of geographic markets (metropolitan or nonmetropolitan) but can self-select the geographic market that they primarily serve. Because applicants choose only one area as "primarily" served, the data do not necessarily capture where CDFIs ultimately make loans and investments or capture CDFIs that self-identify as primarily serving metropolitan areas but also make loans and investments in nonmetropolitan areas. Therefore, we cannot say with certainty that CDFIs invest all of their awards in the areas that they select as their primary geographic markets. In addition, for 2004, data on the primary geographic market for technical assistance applicants were not readily available because the 2004 applications were paper based. As a result, we did not include 100 awardees from 2004 in our data set. In addition to these limitations, the data do not reflect de-obligation of awards completed before May 2008 because the CDFI Fund did not have any electronic system to record de-obligations before that time.

To assess the amounts and number of investments and loans that CDFIs deployed to metropolitan and nonmetropolitan areas, we obtained transaction-level program data. Our review focused on fiscal years 2004 through 2010, for which complete transaction-level data were available for individual transactions (for example, a loan made to a local business) from the Community Investment Impact System (CIIS) database. We obtained aggregate data on the number and dollar amount of loans and investments outstanding, as well as the percentage of transactions and percentage of dollars outstanding by year and metropolitan status. There are two main limitations to the data set. First, the transaction-level data for the CDFI Program represent CDFIs' loans and investments outstanding (to which we also refer as total portfolio outstanding) at the end of each reporting year and reflect CDFI Program awards combined with the CDFIs' other funding sources. Therefore, the data do not allow us to identify which loans and investments resulted directly from CDFI Program awards. In addition, the program does not require certain types of financial institutions (for example, regulated depository institutions such as banks, bank holding companies, and credit unions) to report loan and investment data because bank call reports (quarterly reports that collect basic financial data from commercial banks) already capture this information. Technical assistance awardees also are not required to submit transaction-level reports because these awards are intended for internal capacity-building activities rather than for providing financial and developmental services to the community. However, some of these CDFIs voluntarily submit transaction-level data to the CDFI Fund. For example, program officials stated that in fiscal year 2011, 21 of 37 regulated depository institutions, or about 57 percent, voluntarily submitted these data reports. They also stated that, in general, 70 percent of all financial and technical assistance awardees submitted these reports, as did approximately 85 percent of all financial assistance awardees. But because not all CDFI awardees must report transaction-level data, we cannot generalize the findings to the entire CDFI awardee population.

Analysis of NMTC Program Allocations

The NMTC Program ensures that a proportionate number of applicants that are "rural CDEs"—CDEs that principally serve nonmetropolitan areas—receive tax credits. It also attempts to ensure that at least 20 percent of the aggregate investments made with each round of NMTC allocations are made in eligible nonmetropolitan areas. To describe the extent to which the NMTC Program allocated tax credits to rural CDEs, we reviewed annual allocation reports. To assess the extent to which the NMTC Program has met the proportionality goal for investments in nonmetropolitan areas, we analyzed the total CDE community investments to nonmetropolitan areas for calendar years 2008 through 2011. Using the annual NMTC Program allocation reports, we compiled data on total funding, the number of CDEs making investments in nonmetropolitan areas, and total investments committed to nonmetropolitan areas for the years the policy was in place (from 2008). We calculated the percentage of the total investments committed to nonmetropolitan areas and present the data in terms of calendar years because the program conducts its allocation rounds on a calendar year basis.

To assess the amounts and number of investments and loans that CDEs deployed to metropolitan and nonmetropolitan areas, we analyzed the dollar amount and number of CDE projects financed in metropolitan and nonmetropolitan areas for fiscal years 2003 through 2010. The NMTC Program provided us with aggregate transaction-level data on the total amount of qualified low-income community investment and with the metropolitan statistical area and combined metropolitan statistical area of the project location (MSACMSA code). To sort the data by metropolitan and nonmetropolitan, we created a new variable based on the MSACMSA code. We calculated the percentage of dollars and percentage of community investments for fiscal years 2003 through 2010. We present this information in terms of fiscal years because this is how the NMTC Program collects the data.

For all the analysis on CDFI and NMTC programs, we used data obtained from the CDFI Fund's CIIS and internal certification, application, and award databases. We conducted a reliability assessment of the data by reviewing documentation from the CDFI Fund and its data contractor, Kearney & Company, which maintains and manages the CIIS database. Specifically, we reviewed their processes for ensuring consistent data entry and for addressing potentially inaccurate data. We also interviewed officials from the CDFI Fund to address questions about the reliability of the information and checked the data for extreme values and missing data points. We found the data to be sufficiently reliable for our purposes.

We conducted this performance audit from January to April 2012 in accordance with generally accepted government auditing standards. Those standards require that we plan and perform the audit to obtain sufficient, appropriate evidence to provide a reasonable basis for our findings and conclusions based on our audit objectives. We believe that the evidence obtained provides a reasonable basis for our findings and conclusions based on our audit objectives.

ENCLOSURE II. CERTIFIED CDFIS AND CDES BY STATE OR TERRITORY AS OF FEBRUARY 29, 2012

Figure 6 lists all certified Community Development Financial Institutions (CDFI) and Community Development Entities (CDE) as of February 29, 2012. The numbers of CDEs represent both the applicant CDEs and their subsidiaries, which are legal entities that applicant CDEs own or directly control and to which CDEs can transfer all or part of their allocation authority.

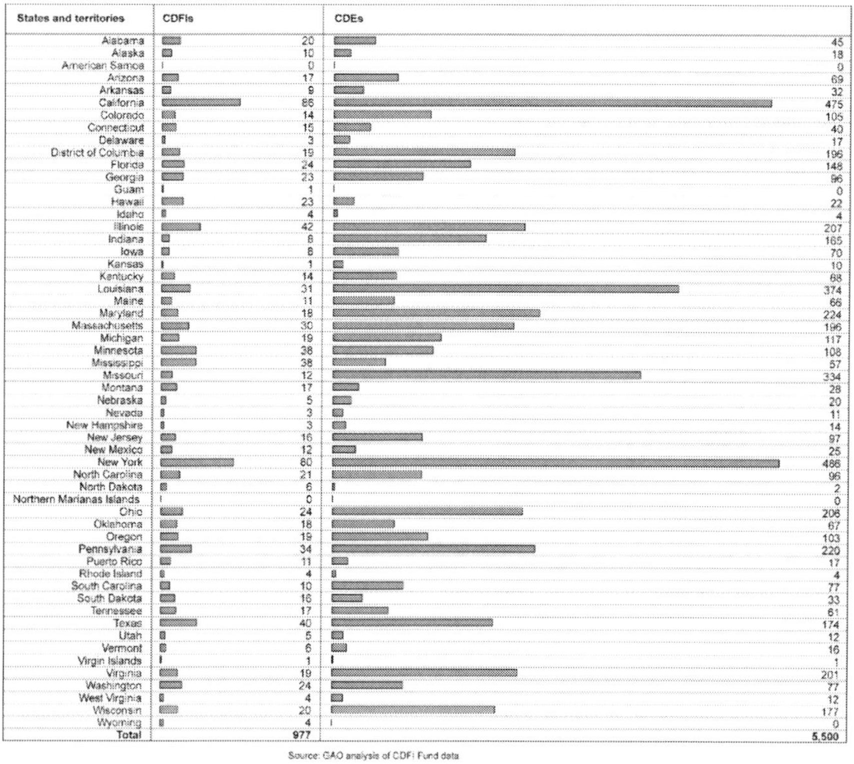

Figure 6. Certified CDFIs and CDEs by State or Territory as of February 29, 2012.

ENCLOSURE III. CDFIS' PERCENTAGES OF TOTAL PORTFOLIOS OUTSTANDING IN NONMETROPOLITAN AREAS BY STATE, FISCAL YEARS 2004-2010

We obtained data from the CDFI Program on the total dollar amount of CDFIs' loans and investments outstanding (also referred to as total portfolio outstanding) by state and metropolitan or nonmetropolitan status for fiscal years 2004 through 2010. Figure 7 represents the percentage of total portfolios outstanding in nonmetropolitan areas in each state over this time period.

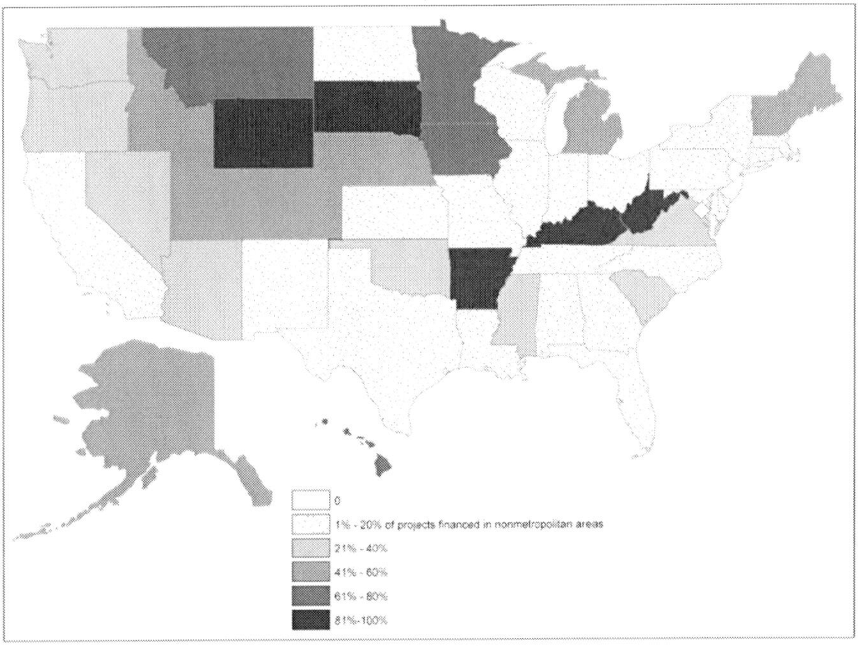

Source: GAO analysis of CDFI fund data; map (MapInfo).

Figure 7. CDFIs' Percentages of Total Portfolios Outstanding in Nonmetropolitan Areas by State, Fiscal Years 2004-2010.

ENCLOSURE IV. CDES' PERCENTAGES OF PROJECTS FINANCED IN NONMETROPOLITAN AREAS BY STATE, FISCAL YEARS 2003-2010

We obtained data from the NMTC Program on the dollar amount of projects financed by CDEs by state and nonmetropolitan status for fiscal years 2004 through 2010. Figure 8 represents the percentage of projects financed in nonmetropolitan areas in each state over this time period.

Source: GAO analysis of CDFI fund data; map (MapInfo).

Figure 8. CDEs' Percentages of Projects Financed in Nonmetropolitan Areas by State, Fiscal Years 2003-2010.

End Notes

[1] The Riegle Community Development and Regulatory Improvement Act of 1994, Pub. L. No. 103-325, 108 Stat. 2160 (1994).

[2] The Community Renewal Tax Relief Act of 2000, Pub. L. No. 106-554, § 121, 114 Stat. 2763 (2000). The Act generally defines low-income communities as census tracts with poverty rates of at least 20 percent or median family incomes of no more than 80 percent of statewide median family income. The NMTC Program generally defines low-income

persons as individuals with income of not more than 80 percent of the area median family income.

[3] A qualified equity investment is any equity investment in a CDE that an investor acquires at its original issue solely in exchange for cash. The CDE must use at least 85 percent of the cash to make investments in NMTC-eligible low-income communities.

[4] The time periods for these data reflect the periods for which public release data were available from the CDFI Fund's Community Investment Impact System. The CDFI and NMTC Programs began making awards in 1994 and 2002, respectively.

[5] Consolidated Appropriations Act of 2012, Pub. L. No. 112-74, 125 Stat. 786 (2012); H.R. Rep. No. 112-136, at 14 (2012).

[6] Although we present CDE transaction-level data on a fiscal year basis, the NMTC Program conducts its allocation rounds on a calendar year basis. Therefore, this report presents NMTC Program allocation data (in other words, information on tax credit allocations the NMTC Program made to CDEs) in terms of calendar years.

[7] Tax Relief and Health Care Act of 2006, Pub. L. No. 109-432, Div. A, Tit. I, § 102(b), 120 Stat. 2922 (2006).

[8] Specifically, such a recipient is one that, over the past 5 years, has dedicated at least 50 percent of its direct financing dollars to nonmetropolitan counties and has committed in its application to dedicate at least 50 percent of its future NMTC direct financing dollars to such areas. The recipient is not required to be physically located in a nonmetropolitan area to be designated as such.

[9] Subsidiary CDEs are legal entities that applicant CDEs own or directly control and to which CDEs can transfer all or part of their allocation authority.

[10] Financial assistance can be in the form of grants, loans, credit union shares, equity investments, and deposits to CDFIs. However, most financial assistance awards are in the form of grants. Investment areas and targeted populations are defined in 12 C.F.R. § 1805.201(b)(3).

[11] CDEs make community investments with the proceeds of qualified equity investments from outside investors. The community investments can include any capital or equity investments in, or loans to, qualified active low-income community businesses; loans purchased from other CDEs; financial counseling and other services to qualified active low-income community businesses, or to residents of a low-income community; or equity investments in, or loans to, other CDEs. For more information about the NMTC investment process, see GAO, *New Markets Tax Credit: The Credit Helps Fund a Variety of Projects in Low-Income Communities, but Could Be Simplified*, GAO-10-334 (Washington, D.C.: Jan. 29, 2010).

[12] See S. 996, 112th Cong. (2011); H.R. 2655, 112th Cong. (2011); Office of Management and Budget, Executive Office of the President, Fiscal Year 2013 Budget of the U.S. Government (2012).

[13] According to the CDFI Fund, a major urban area is a metropolitan statistical area with a population equal to or greater than 1 million, including both central city and surrounding suburbs. A minor urban area is a metropolitan statistical area with a population of more than 50,000 and less than 1 million, including both central city and surrounding suburbs. A rural area is any area not contained in a major or minor urban area.

[14] See OMB Bulletin No. 99-04.

[15] See enclosure I for more detail on how we classified geographic areas in this report.

[16] U.S. Census Bureau, Core Based Statistical Area (CBSA) Status for the United States, Regions, and Divisions, and for Puerto Rico: 2010 and 2011, CBSA-EST2011-12 (Washington, D.C.: April 2012).

[17] 12 CFR §1805.700(d).

[18] While not within the scope of this report, the CDFI Fund's Native American CDFI Assistance Program provides similar awards to CDFIs and organizations that serve economically distressed Native communities. According to the CDFI Fund, these organizations serve mostly rural communities. In 2009, the CDFI Fund also implemented a Capacity Building

Initiative to provide technical assistance and training opportunities for CDFIs. The initiative also focuses on extending CDFI coverage to underserved communities, including a specialized focus in rural areas.

[19] Pub. L. No. 109-432, Div. A, Tit. I, § 102(b).

[20] The NMTC Program applies the 1999 Office of Management and Budget bulletin definition of nonmetropolitan areas to 2000 data to determine eligibility. According to this classification system, 19.6 percent of the U.S. population lived in nonmetropolitan counties in 2000.

[21] The NMTC Program's review process is similar to the CDFI program's review process; see figure 1.

[22] For a more-detailed description of the criteria used to evaluate NMTC Program applications, see GAO, *New Markets Tax Credit: Minority Entities Are Less Successful in Obtaining Awards Than Non-Minority Entities*, GAO-09-536 (Washington, D.C., Apr. 30, 2009).

[23] GAO.

[24] Under IRC §45D(g)(3), there is a recapture provision by which an investor can lose the right to claim the NMTC if certain conditions are not met throughout the seven-year period after the qualified equity investment is made. In its February 6, 2012 response to the CDFI Fund's Request for Public Comments on the NMTC Program, Novogradac and Company stated on behalf of the NMTC Working Group that the recapture provision increases transaction costs and discourages investments in specific types of businesses, including non-real estate businesses. The Internal Revenue Service recently indicated that non-real estate investments may be smaller than real estate investments, and it has proposed regulations that would modify the NMTC Program to facilitate and encourage investments in non-real-estate businesses in low-income communities. In addition, it requested comments on potential regulatory changes that would simplify the substantiation requirements in cases where CDEs invest qualified equity investment proceeds in other CDEs that then make smaller (i.e., less than $250,000) loans to non-real-estate businesses in low-income communities.

[25] From fiscal years 2004 through 2010, the CDFI program awarded a total of $436 million, of which approximately $414 million (95 percent) was in financial assistance awards and $23 million (5 percent) was in technical assistance awards. Dollar amounts have been rounded.

[26] Amounts do not sum to $436 million because of rounding. As part of the CDFI application for combined financial and technical awards, applicants select the primary geographic market they serve, although they may also serve a combination of metropolitan and nonmetropolitan markets.

[27] According to CDFI Fund officials, the Fund does not require certain types of financial institutions (for example, regulated depository institutions such as banks, bank holding companies, and credit unions) to report loan and investment data because call reports capture this information. In addition, technical assistance awardees are not required to submit detailed data because these awards are to be used for internal capacity-building activities rather than for financial and developmental services to the community. However, some of these awardees voluntarily submit the data to the CDFI Fund. For example, CDFI Fund officials stated that in fiscal year 2011, 21 of 37 regulated depository institutions, or about 57 percent, voluntarily submitted these data reports. They also stated that, in general, 70 percent of all financial and technical assistance awardees submit these reports, as do approximately 85 percent of all financial assistance awardees.

[28] The number of projects that CDEs financed in nonmetropolitan areas from fiscal years 2003 through 2010 remained relatively steady as a percentage of all projects financed (approximately 17 percent).

[29] According to the CDFI Fund, a major urban area is a metropolitan statistical area with a population equal to or greater than 1 million, including both central city and surrounding suburbs. A minor urban area is a metropolitan statistical area with a population of more than 50,000 and less than 1 million, including both central city and surrounding suburbs. A rural area is any area not contained in a major or minor urban area. In the NMTC Program

application, applicants must indicate whether they serve major urban, minor urban, or nonmetropolitan areas.

[30] The SECA category allows CDFIs with assets of less than a certain amount or in operation for fewer than 5 years to apply separately from larger and more established (regular) CDFIs. From fiscal years 2004 through 2010, SECA applicants received approximately 13 percent of the total dollar amount of financial assistance awards, while regular applicants received approximately 87 percent of financial assistance funding.

In: The Community Development …
Editor: Andre L. Wright
ISBN: 978-1-62417-551-0

Chapter 4

TESTIMONY OF DONNA J. GAMBRELL, DIRECTOR, CDFI FUND. HEARING ON "COMMUNITY DEVELOPMENT FINANCIAL INSTITUTIONS (CDFIS): THEIR UNIQUE ROLE AND CHALLENGES SERVING LOWER-INCOME, UNDERSERVED AND MINORITY COMMUNITIES"*

INTRODUCTION

Good afternoon Chairman Frank, Ranking Member Bachus, and the distinguished Members of the House Financial Services Committee. My name is Donna J. Gambrell, and I am the Director of the U.S. Department of the Treasury's Community Development Financial Institutions Fund—known as the CDFI Fund. I am truly honored to be here today to speak before you about the CDFI Fund and our role in helping to promote economic recovery in these challenging times.

Since its founding in 1994, the CDFI Fund has been committed to creating opportunity in disadvantaged communities. But in the past year there has been a growing recognition that the work of the CDFI Fund—and of the more than 800 certified CDFIs across the nation—is more important than ever. The

* This is an edited, reformatted and augmented version of the testimony given on March 9, 2010 before the House Financial Services Committee.

financial crisis has only magnified the daunting challenges that low-income communities have long faced, and the CDFI Fund has been called upon to expand its work and to play a larger role in promoting economic recovery in communities that have been hardest hit by the recession.

I am pleased to report that the CDFI Fund has served with distinction in answering that call. In my testimony today I will outline the many ways in which, since the beginning of the recession, the CDFI Fund has worked to build small businesses and to create jobs in low-income communities, to develop affordable housing, and to expand the capacity of community-based social service organizations, such as community healthcare centers. I will also look at some of new proposed initiatives we hope to undertake in the coming year to ensure that the recovery that is now under way will be shared by all.

Above all, I would like to assure the Members of this Committee that the CDFI Fund is more than prepared to continue answering the call. We are uniquely positioned to serve low-income and economically distressed communities. We have welcomed every new responsibility with which we have been entrusted in the past year, and we will welcome every new responsibility going forward. Just last week I spoke before the Congressional Black Caucus, which includes 10 Members of this Committee, to share with them the same important message: The CDFI Fund stands ready to play an even greater role in bringing economic opportunity to those who need it most.

THE WORK OF THE CDFI FUND

I would like to begin by providing a brief overview of the origins and the work of the CDFI Fund.

In the early 1990s, Congress recognized that many of the critical social problems facing our nation's distressed urban, rural, and Native American communities were caused in part by a host of crippling economic problems—stagnant economic growth, widespread unemployment and deep poverty, inadequate financial access and education, and the lack of economic opportunity. To address these issues, Congress in 1994 enacted the Riegle Community Development and Regulatory Improvement Act (P.L. 103-325), which included a provision that established the CDFI Fund.

The mission of the CDFI Fund is to promote economic revitalization and community development through an investment and assistance program for Community Development Financial Institutions (CDFIs). CDFIs are community-based financial institutions that specialize in serving low-income people and economically distressed communities. There are four main types:

- **Community development banks** are for-profit corporations that provide capital to rebuild economically distressed communities through targeted lending and investment. Of CDFI banks, 54 percent are defined by the FDIC as Minority Depository Institutions, indicating that these banks are minority-owned or are focused on serving the needs of a minority community;
- **Community development credit unions** are member-owned non-profit cooperatives that promote ownership of assets and savings, and provide affordable credit and retail financial services to low-income people;
- **Community development loan funds** (usually non-profits) provide financing and development services to businesses, organizations, and individuals in low-income urban and rural areas, and can be further categorized based on the type of client served: micro-enterprise, small business, housing, and community service organizations; and
- **Community development venture capital funds** include both for-profit and non-profit organizations that provide equity and debt-with-equity features for businesses in distressed communities.

CDFIs typically offer loan rates and terms that are more flexible than those offered by traditional financial institutions. They also provide financial services—such as technical assistance for small businesses, and home buying and credit counseling for consumers—that help to ensure that borrowers use credit effectively.

The CDFI Fund currently seeks to build the capacity of CDFIs through a number of programs, including:

- **CDFI Financial and Technical Assistance**-Provides capital grants to certified CDFIs, which in turn provide loans, investments, financial services (including financial education) and technical assistance to underserved populations and low-income communities; also provides technical assistance grants to certified CDFIs and entities that will become certified as CDFIs within three years.
- **Native Initiatives**-Provides financial assistance awards, technical assistance grants, and training to CDFIs created specifically to serve

Native Communities and to other Native entities proposing to become or create Native CDFIs.

- **Bank Enterprise Award**-Provides monetary awards to FDIC-insured banks to increase their investment in low-income communities and/or in CDFIs. The CDFI Fund is proposing not to fund the BEA in FY 2011. Instead, the CDFI Fund will evaluate the enhancements made to the BEA in FY 2009 and FY 2010 and apply this analysis to future funding decisions.
- **New Markets Tax Credit**-Provides tax allocation authority to certified Community Development Entities (CDEs), enabling investors to claim tax credits against their federal income taxes; the CDEs in turn use the capital raised to make investments in low-income communities.
- **Capital Magnet Fund**-Authorized under the Housing and Economic Recovery Act of 2008, the Capital Magnet Fund provides a source of funding for CDFIs and other non-profits to finance the development, rehabilitation, and purchase of affordable housing for low-income persons. The CDFI Fund is proposing not to fund the CMF in FY2011. Treasury will undertake a careful review of the impact of FY2010 funding, and future resource decisions will be informed by this review.

Since its creation in 1994, the CDFI Fund has made more than $1.1 billion in awards to CDFIs. As of December 18, 2009, there were 824 certified CDFIs. During FY 2009, 55 new CDFIs were certified, 14 more than were certified in the prior year. This increase in the number of certified CDFIs will no doubt increase the number of applications in future funding years.

The CDFI Fund's Expanded Role in the Economic Recovery

In the current environment there is a renewed discussion of the importance of community development finance and its role in promoting economic recovery. The result of this discussion is that CDFIs have been asked to play a critical role in helping to revitalize the nation's economy. Indeed, President Obama views the CDFI industry as a key part of his strategy to address the financial crisis, and Congress and the Administration have taken major steps to expand the CDFI Fund's mission and impact.

The first of these steps was the passage of the American Recovery and Reinvestment Act on February 17, 2009. The Recovery Act provided the CDFI Fund extra funding—$100 million beyond our annual appropriation for fiscal year (FY) 2009—to enhance the lending capacity of CDFIs. The new legislation also contained an additional $3 billion of New Markets Tax Credit allocation authority. In addition, the Administration supported strong levels of funding for the CDFI Fund in FY 2010.

We at the CDFI Fund have been mindful of the tremendous responsibility that we have been given in the midst of the financial crisis, and we have worked tirelessly to ensure that we implement the Administration's agenda as quickly and effectively as possible. Our key accomplishments in 2009 include:

- **Rapid disbursement of Recovery Act resources** – Less than 100 days after the enactment of the Recovery Act, the CDFI Fund announced financial assistance awards through the Recovery Act to 59 CDFIs and to 10 Native CDFIs. Just two months later—in record time— we disbursed all $98 million available for grants from the Recovery Act to these CDFIs.
- In addition to disbursing the Recovery Act awards, we made 193 financial and technical assistance awards totaling $160.8 million (compared to 118 awards totaling $62.4 million in FY 2008) through our CDFI and Native American CDFI Assistance (NACA) programs. We also solicited and reviewed over 200 additional applications through supplemental NACA and CDFI financial and technical assistance award rounds in FY 2009.
- **Creation of a new Advisory Board Subcommittee** – As the financial crisis deepened in late 2008, Bill Bynum, the Chairman of the Community Development Advisory Board and CEO of the Enterprise Corporation of the Delta, and I agreed to form a new Advisory Board Subcommittee to assess the impact of the crisis on the institutions that the CDFI Fund supports and to offer policy recommendations to increase that support. The Subcommittee presented its recommendations in March 2009, and the CDFI Fund has made significant progress in implementing those recommendations. For example, in July 2009 we created a new Office of Training and Outreach that focuses on expanding training and outreach by coordinating activities with government and non-

governmental organizations interested in improving conditions in low-income communities.

- **Enhancement of key business processes** – In 2009, we made several administrative changes designed to enable us to get funds more quickly than ever to the communities that need them. We now make decisions on all new applications for CDFI and CDE certification within 90 days after we receive them. We send out assistance agreements on the same day we make award announcements. And on average we now disburse awards—a process which used to take over 12 months—in 60 days.
- **Launch of a new Capacity-Building Initiative** – This new initiative seeks to ensure the growth and sustainability of CDFIs by providing expanded technical assistance and training opportunities. Among its key components:
  - **Assistance for specialized CDFIs** – Enables CDFIs to grow their capacity to address complex problems in their specialized markets, and helps to establish new CDFIs in markets where financial institutions have not historically existed.
  - **Affordable housing lending** – Provides assistance to CDFIs in identifying the best strategies for restructuring troubled loans, as well as developing new lines of business.
  - **Small business lending** – Helps CDFIs that make small business loans—and that may be seeing their clients struggle or even disappear—develop adequate resources and new lines of business.
  - **CDFI business process** – Provides technical assistance to enable CDFIs to manage their portfolios, to minimize risk, to address liquidity and capitalization issues, and to expand into new markets.
- **Launch of a new Community Development Capital Initiative** – This new initiative gives certified CDFI banks, thrifts, and credit unions access to capital investments under the Emergency Economic Stabilization Act at a dividend rate of two percent for the first eight years and nine percent thereafter. This new initiative will offer affordable capital to CDFIs across the country, which will help expand the offering of credit to small businesses seeking to expand and to create jobs.

The Impact of CDFIs

The financial crisis has presented extraordinary challenges to our nation's distressed communities. The entire nation is living and working in a new and uncertain environment.

The CDFI Fund and the CDFI industry have chosen to accept this new environment as it is—as something not simply to endure but to face head on, to understand, and to navigate as skillfully and effectively as possible. I do not want to minimize the challenges confronting the CDFI industry in the wake of the economic downturn, but I most certainly believe that there is another side to the story, a very positive side. Indeed, I can assure you that, despite the very real challenges it presents, the new economic environment has offered very real opportunities for CDFIs to expand their impact in the communities they serve.

I am pleased to report that the CDFI industry has made exceptional progress in realizing those opportunities. Consider the accomplishments of CDFI Fund awardees reported in 2009:

Performance of CDFI Awardees During 2008	
1. Number of Full Time Jobs Created or Maintained (77)*	70,260
2. Number of Small Businesses Financed (104)*	10,792
3. Number of Commercial Real Estate Properties Financed (55)*	1,676
4. Number of Affordable Housing Units Financed (22)*	2,133
5. Number of Homebuyers Who Obtain Financing (50)*	1,998
6. Number of Accounts Opened to the Unbanked (11)*	4,235
7. Dollars, in millions, Leveraged with Private Investments*	$1,298
8. Number of Individuals Provided with Financial Literacy and Other Training (126)*	159,546
9. Individual Development Accounts (IDAs) Provided by CDFIs (53)*	6,478
10. Dollar amount, in millions, of IDAs (54)*	$5.86

* Numbers in parentheses are the number of CDFI Program awardees reporting on this particular measure.

Our industry's performance in 2008 speaks volumes about its resilience, commitment, and creativity. At the same time, however, I would like to encourage everyone who reviews our record to look beyond the statistics, for there is much more to the story than numbers alone. Each business financed, each job created, each home purchased, each Individual Development Account opened represents a critical step in the transformation of a life, a family, and a community.

After all, that's what our work is really about. It's not just about creating programs and providing services; these are just the means to a greater end. It's about changing lives and building stronger, more productive communities. And that's why we keep working every day to do what we do even better.

CDFIs as Innovators

But CDFIs are not only focused on transforming lives and communities. They are also helping to transform the financial services industry by creating innovative financing tools to serve the unique needs of their clients. Let me give you just a few examples of the CDFI industry's capacity for innovation.

The Montana Community Development Corporation (MCDC), a CDFI based in Missoula, is known for working on complex, multi-partner deals with "triple bottom line" impact. In one such deal, MCDC was the coordinator of a loan to a 100-year old dairy. The loan financed a $1.2 million methane digester that has enabled the dairy to recycle 100 percent of its waste into fertilizer, and has turned the dairy into an environmental leader. Eventually the dairy plans to sell Carbon Credits. MCDC led the project with its own financing as well as funds from two economic development groups, two banks, and four federal grant programs. Montana Senator Jon Tester recently recognized this effort as one of the leading triple bottom line economic development projects in the state.

The Reinvestment Fund (TRF) is another CDFI exploring ways to promote "green" values. The Philadelphia-based organization partnered with The Food Trust, a nonprofit dedicated to making healthy food available to all, to develop and implement a sustainable energy model for supermarkets in underserved communities in Philadelphia. The initiative recently completed a small grocery store demonstration project with energy audits and a revenue tracking system, and is now working with TRF's supermarket financing program to identify sites for large, neighborhood green supermarkets. As result of this initiative, TRF is able to help new and existing supermarkets identify and evaluate energy efficiency measures, such as high-efficiency lighting and refrigeration equipment, which can translate into savings.

One more example: the New Hampshire Community Loan Fund, in Concord, NH, was founded in 1984 to use capital and technical assistance to help people change their lives. The organization made its first loan to thirteen families facing eviction from their manufactured housing park when the park's owner decided to sell the property to condominium developers. The loan enabled the families to buy the park and manage it as a cooperative. It also launched the Community Loan Fund's Manufactured Housing Park Program, which, since 1984, has helped more than 5,000 families and individuals from 93 manufactured housing parks throughout New Hampshire to buy the land beneath their homes and convert their parks to cooperative ownership. The program offers an outstanding example of what can happen when a CDFI keeps its eyes open and works hard to develop innovative solutions to the problems in the communities it serves.

These are just three examples of the quality of innovation to be found at CDFIs. While these three organizations may seem exceptional, I can assure you that they are anything but rare. Our industry is filled with innovators who are dedicated to developing uncommon solutions to pressing economic problems. And I believe that this spirit of innovation can help to bring about an economic recovery that is strong and stable and shared by all Americans.

MOVING FORWARD TOGETHER

As we celebrate the 15th anniversary of the creation of the CDFI Fund, this is an opportune time not just to reflect on what the CDFI Fund has accomplished but also to look forward to envision the next steps we can take to create opportunity in our nation's most distressed communities.

We have recently released a request for public comments and plan to take a holistic review of our entire authorizing statute, looking not only at technical and substantive revisions to existing provisions, but also at provisions that have not yet been exercised. As an important part of this process we will also hold listening sessions with CDFIs across the country to discuss the community economic development challenges they face and to get insight firsthand from the communities they serve. The information we gather from the public comments and listening sessions will no doubt guide us as we develop plans for the CDFI Fund's future.

But some of our next steps are already clear. The President's FY 2011 Budget builds on the CDFI Fund's recent momentum by requesting $250 million in funding, including resources for two new exciting initiatives in which the CDFI Fund will play a key role. The first of these is the Bank on USA initiative that will help expand access to mainstream financial services to help families avoid predatory lending traps and high fees for check-cashing and other alternative financial services. The initiative will promote broader access to bank accounts, basic credit products, and other financial services to help these families build savings and solid credit histories. The FY 2011 Budget proposes $50 million to establish for the Bank on USA initiative.

The President's FY 2011 Budget also provides funding for a second new initiative—the Healthy Food Financing Initiative, which is a new multi-year, multi-agency effort to increase the availability of affordable, healthy foods in underserved urban and rural communities. Forming a pillar of First Lady Michelle Obama's *Let's Move!* campaign to solve the epidemic of childhood obesity within a generation, the initiative will emphasize the development or equipping of grocery stores and other healthy food retailers. The USDA, HHS, and Treasury will provide funding to organizations with sound strategies for providing healthy foods to underserved markets. The initiative includes $250 million in New Markets Tax Credit investment authority, $25 million in grants to CDFIs, and technical assistance to help finance businesses dedicated to achieving the goals of the initiative.

The budget also includes an extension of New Markets Tax Credit and important enhancements to the credit. The NMTC attracts investments by allowing investors to claim a 39 percent credit against their federal income taxes in return for making equity investments in Treasury certified Community Development Entities (CDEs), which in turn invest in businesses and real estate projects that serve distressed communities. The FY2011 Budget requests $5 billion in NMTC authority in both 2010 and 2011 and is also proposes that the NMTC be used to offset not only investors' regular federal income taxes but also the taxes they owe under the Alternative Minimum Tax (AMT), and that AMT relief should apply to all NMTC investments that have yet to be made, whether from prior allocation rounds or from the 2010 and future rounds.

Applying AMT relief to all future NMTC investments will attract new private investors that will help strengthen the current market for NMTC credits that have already been allocated, and would establish a clear and consistent policy that would eliminate confusion among investors. If enacted, this proposal would enable the NMTC to speed recovery in the hardest hit communities by greatly increasing its ability to attract private investors.

These are just three steps that we hope to begin in 2010. We must also continue our strong commitment to help CDFIs expand the critical work they do supporting recovery in distressed communities across the country.

Not long ago I was in a meeting with Representative Danny Davis and he said to me, "My District is an island of need looking for a sea of opportunity."

There are many islands of need out there today, many looking for a sea of opportunity that in the past year has become more difficult than ever to find.

But I believe that there is real hope for these communities. There is real hope because CDFIs and the CDFI Fund are committed to ensuring that economic development and job growth reach the communities that need them most. In 2010 and beyond, we will continue building partnerships with other government and non-governmental organizations that are dedicated to strengthening low-income communities. And we will do our very best to bring economic opportunity to each and every island of need in the nation.

On behalf of the CDFI Fund, I would like to express our gratitude for the support of Congress and the Financial Services Committee. We look forward to continuing to work with you in the future.

INDEX

A

access, 4, 5, 8, 12, 16, 18, 25, 58, 60, 62, 66, 68, 105, 110, 113
accountability, 8, 52, 66
accounting, 58, 59
agencies, xi, 3, 4, 31, 34, 38, 45
Alaska, 16, 37
American Recovery and Reinvestment Act, 39, 84, 88, 89, 107
American Recovery and Reinvestment Act of 2009, 39, 89
appropriations, ix, x, 2, 5, 6, 17, 20, 24, 35, 38, 43
Appropriations Act, 21, 35
assessment, 32, 45, 58, 59, 96
assets, 41, 42, 46, 68, 71, 75, 83, 102, 105
audit, 46, 64, 96
audits, 112
authority, xii, 6, 7, 12, 16, 18, 20, 24, 43, 49, 50, 51, 54, 55, 56, 57, 58, 59, 62, 96, 100, 106, 108, 114

B

bank holding companies, 94, 101
banking, 32, 44
banks, ix, 1, 4, 21, 23, 34, 45, 94, 101, 105, 106, 109, 111
barriers, 15
BEA, 8, 12, 21, 22, 23, 42, 106
benchmarks, 76
benefits, xi, 3, 8, 15, 26, 27, 29, 58, 75
board members, 6, 15
bonds, 23, 24
borrowers, 32, 106
budgetary resources, 31
Bureau of Labor Statistics, 13
business processes, 109
business strategy, 54, 76
businesses, ix, x, 1, 2, 3, 4, 10, 14, 19, 20, 24, 26, 27, 32, 50, 54, 56, 58, 68, 77, 78, 100, 101, 105, 106, 114
buyers, 36

C

capacity building, 62
case study, 23
cash, 62, 99
casinos, 54
Catalog of Federal Domestic Assistance, 40, 43
category a, 102
Census, 14, 100
certification, 8, 10, 12, 16, 35, 38, 66, 67, 72, 92, 96, 109
CFR, 39, 42, 100

challenges, ix, 1, 32, 58, 78, 81, 104, 110, 113
Chicago, 33
childhood, 113
citizens, 6
City, 38
classification, 101
clients, 36, 109, 111
Clinton Administration, 11
color, v
commercial, ix, x, 1, 3, 5, 14, 22, 68, 94
commercial bank, 94
Community development financial institutions (CDFIs), ix, x, 1, 3
Community Development Financial Institutions Fund, i, iii, x, xi, 2, 5, 7, 10, 11, 37, 38, 39, 40, 41, 42, 43, 45, 46, 47, 49, 50, 103
community service, 35, 105
complement, 32
complexity, 20
compliance, 51, 52, 55, 76, 81
computer, 75
conflict, 33
conflict of interest, 33
Congress, v, ix, x, xii, 1, 2, 6, 16, 17, 18, 20, 23, 25, 31, 34, 36, 38, 39, 40, 41, 43, 44, 45, 46, 47, 49, 50, 51, 55, 56, 57, 59, 65, 68, 72, 76, 104, 107, 115
congressional interest, x, 2, 5
consensus, 28
Consolidated Appropriations Act, 18, 40, 63, 99
consulting, 15
consumers, 5, 106
copyright, v
Copyright, v
cost, 23, 26, 28, 43, 44, 50, 58
counseling, 8, 17, 36, 51, 54, 62, 66, 68, 100, 106
covering, 19, 53
creativity, 111
credit market, 58

D

damages, v
data set, 94
database, 63, 94, 96
Delta, 108
denial, 6, 66
Department of Agriculture, 18
Department of Health and Human Services, 18
Department of the Treasury, x, xi, 2, 20, 40, 41, 42, 47, 49, 62
depository institutions, 40, 94, 101
deposits, 11, 21, 100
depth, 42
development assistance, xi, 2, 25, 31
development banks, ix, x, 2, 3, 4, 62, 71, 105
directors, 6
disaster, 32
disaster relief, 32
disbursement, 108
distribution, 18, 58, 91
District of Columbia, 8, 59
diversity, 73, 75, 82, 93
Dodd-Frank Wall Street Reform XE "Reform" and Consumer Protection Act, 25
draft, 33, 91

E

economic activity, xi, 2, 5, 11, 27, 28, 29, 31, 44
economic challenges, ix, 1
economic development, x, 2, 3, 5, 22, 24, 25, 27, 28, 29, 31, 35, 43, 111, 113, 115
economic development policies, xi, 2, 25, 27, 28
economic downturn, 110
economic growth, 54, 105

economic problem, 105, 112
economic theory, 29
economic well-being, 30
education, 22, 25, 36, 43, 47, 105, 106
eligibility criteria, ix, x, 2, 8, 17, 24, 47
Emergency Economic Stabilization Act, 59, 110
empirical studies, 30
employees, 27, 75
employers, 30
employment, xi, 3, 27, 29, 30
employment opportunities, 29
empowerment, 27
energy, 5, 112
energy efficiency, 112
England, 46
entrepreneurs, 5
entrepreneurship, 27
environment, 107, 110
epidemic, 113
equipment, 15, 68, 75, 112
equity, xi, 4, 8, 11, 19, 20, 21, 31, 49, 50, 53, 54, 59, 60, 62, 65, 68, 76, 78, 89, 99, 100, 101, 106, 114
evidence, 23, 64, 96
executive branch, 45
expenditures, 26
externalities, 26

F

families, 15, 112, 113
family income, 19, 53, 99
Fannie Mae, 35
FDIC, 21, 22, 105, 106
FEC, 36, 47
federal assistance, xi, 3
federal funds, 59
federal government, 18, 60
Federal Register, 40, 41, 42
Federal Reserve, 4, 38, 44, 46
financial, ix, x, 1, 2, 3, 4, 6, 8, 10, 12, 13, 14, 16, 17, 22, 24, 25, 32, 35, 36, 44, 47, 51, 54, 60, 62, 63, 65, 66, 67, 69, 72, 75, 82, 83, 91, 93, 94, 100, 101, 102, 104, 105, 106, 107, 108, 109, 110, 111, 113
financial condition, 35
financial crisis, 104, 107, 108, 110
financial data, 94
financial institutions, ix, x, 1, 2, 3, 6, 12, 22, 44, 62, 66, 91, 94, 101, 105, 106, 109
financial markets, 33
fiscal year 2009, 72
food, 17, 18, 112, 114
Food and Drug Administration, 21
foreclosure, 17
formula, 21, 78
Freddie Mac, 35
fringe benefits, 71
funding, 7, 12, 16, 17, 18, 23, 24, 25, 31, 32, 33, 35, 36, 38, 39, 51, 55, 63, 65, 68, 69, 73, 75, 76, 82, 84, 87, 91, 92, 93, 94, 95, 102, 106, 107, 113
funds, ix, x, 2, 4, 13, 14, 15, 16, 17, 25, 32, 34, 35, 39, 40, 42, 55, 57, 62, 63, 65, 69, 71, 72, 81, 91, 105, 109, 111

G

GAO, xii, 9, 20, 22, 23, 31, 34, 36, 41, 42, 45, 46, 47, 58, 60, 61, 63, 67, 83, 88, 91, 100, 101
General Accounting Office, 46
governance, 46
government policy, 26
Government Sponsored Enterprises, 47
governments, 8, 66
grant programs, 33, 111
grants, 11, 14, 15, 16, 18, 21, 33, 35, 36, 60, 100, 106, 108, 114
grouping, 84, 93
growth, 27, 28, 82, 109, 115
GSEs, 35
guidance, 22, 34, 91

H

Hawaii, 16, 36, 37
HHS, 18, 31, 114
hiring, 27, 29
history, ix, x, 2, 5, 13, 63
homebuyers, ix, x, 1, 2, 3, 10, 32, 36
homes, 112
host, 104
House, 16, 17, 18, 23, 24, 25, 32, 33, 38, 40, 41, 43, 45, 46, 47, 62, 63, 103
House of Representatives, 62
House Report, 63
housing, 5, 14, 22, 24, 35, 36, 104, 105, 107, 109, 112
Housing and Urban Development, 6, 31, 59
HUD, 6, 31, 34, 36, 38
human, 5
human development, 5
Hurricane Katrina, 59, 60
hurricanes, 60

I

improvements, 5
income, ix, x, xi, 1, 2, 3, 5, 8, 10, 12, 14, 15, 17, 18, 19, 20, 24, 28, 30, 31, 43, 49, 50, 51, 52, 53, 54, 55, 56, 57, 58, 59, 60, 62, 66, 68, 95, 99, 100, 101, 104, 105, 106, 107, 109, 114, 115
income tax, xi, 49, 106, 114
Indian reservation, 13, 14, 15
individual development, 22
individuals, xi, 2, 4, 5, 8, 12, 14, 19, 24, 25, 30, 56, 60, 99, 105, 112
industries, 28
industry, 107, 110, 111, 112
inflation, 57
injury, v
institutions, ix, x, 1, 2, 3, 4, 32, 62, 95, 101, 108
interagency coordination, 34
intermediaries, 4, 52, 62
Internal Revenue Service, 41, 55, 101
intervention, 17
investment, x, xi, 2, 8, 11, 13, 15, 18, 19, 21, 23, 26, 28, 31, 43, 49, 50, 51, 52, 53, 55, 57, 59, 60, 62, 66, 67, 68, 76, 81, 87, 88, 94, 95, 99, 100, 101, 105, 106, 114
investment capital, 8, 19, 66
investment size, 81
investments, ix, x, xi, 1, 3, 8, 10, 18, 19, 21, 22, 23, 24, 27, 30, 34, 49, 50, 52, 53, 54, 55, 56, 58, 59, 60, 62, 63, 65, 67, 68, 76, 77, 78, 79, 82, 83, 85, 87, 88, 92, 94, 95, 97, 99, 100, 101, 106, 107, 110, 114
investors, x, 2, 4, 8, 10, 18, 19, 20, 26, 28, 32, 50, 52, 53, 54, 55, 58, 60, 62, 68, 78, 100, 106, 114
IRC, 101
islands, 114
issues, ix, x, 2, 16, 46, 51, 105, 109

J

job creation, 14
jurisdiction, 51
justification, 43

L

laws, 51, 63, 91
laws and regulations, 91
lead, 28
leadership, 6
legislation, 5, 23, 34, 41, 58, 64, 68, 75, 108
legislative proposals, 45
lending, xi, 3, 4, 14, 15, 21, 23, 24, 32, 40, 44, 105, 108, 109, 113
limited liability, 21

liquidity, 14, 32, 109
literacy, 12
loan guarantees, 35, 43
loans, ix, x, 1, 3, 8, 11, 14, 21, 22, 24, 32, 35, 43, 51, 53, 60, 62, 63, 65, 67, 68, 82, 83, 85, 92, 93, 94, 95, 97, 100, 101, 106, 109
local government, 13
Louisiana, 60
low-income communities (LICs), x, 2, 8, 18, 51

M

major purchases, 36
majority, 33, 46, 52, 65, 66, 81
management, xi, 3, 5, 25, 31, 33, 34, 35, 45, 54, 76
manufactured housing, 112
mapping, 39
materials, 8, 15, 77
matter, v
median, 19, 53, 99
membership, 21
methodology, 23, 44, 64
metropolitan areas, 13, 20, 65, 77, 81, 82, 83, 88, 92, 94
Mexico, 37
migration, 53
mission, xi, 3, 8, 10, 16, 36, 51, 56, 62, 66, 105, 107
missions, 34
models, 45
momentum, 113
Montana, 37, 111

N

naming, 33
Native communities, 64, 75, 100
New Markets Tax Credit (NMTC), xi, 6, 18, 41, 49, 50, 62, 91
NOAA, 41
non-refundable tax credit, xi, 19, 41, 49

O

Obama, 7, 16, 18, 23, 25, 46, 113
Obama Administration, 7, 16, 18, 23, 25, 46
obesity, 113
objectivity, 33
Office of Management and Budget, 31, 45, 59, 60, 69, 100, 101
officials, 64, 65, 66, 69, 70, 73, 75, 76, 77, 81, 82, 87, 92, 93, 95, 96, 101
Oklahoma, 16, 37, 38
OMB, 31, 32, 45, 100
operations, 17, 21, 29, 68
opportunities, 4, 17, 52, 100, 109, 110
opportunity costs, 58
outreach, 8, 66, 109
overlap, 31, 59
ownership, 105, 112

P

participants, 27
payroll, 29
permission, v
Philadelphia, 112
policy, x, 2, 5, 11, 24, 25, 27, 29, 30, 33, 43, 57, 60, 76, 87, 89, 95, 108, 114
policymakers, 28, 29
population, 4, 13, 19, 53, 60, 64, 69, 76, 95, 100, 101, 102
portfolio, 63, 81, 83, 94, 97
positive externalities, 26
poverty, 8, 13, 14, 19, 27, 53, 66, 99, 105
preparation, v
present value, 59
President, 5, 6, 7, 25, 31, 34, 38, 40, 42, 43, 45, 46, 100, 107, 113
President Clinton, 5, 46

President Obama, 25, 34, 107
private investment, xi, 3, 5, 18
probability, 20
producers, 30
profit, ix, x, 1, 3, 4, 52, 105
project, 81, 96, 111, 112
proportionality, 20, 65, 73, 75, 76, 77, 79, 81, 87, 89, 92, 93, 95
proposed regulations, 101
public service, 31
Puerto Rico, 8, 9, 59, 100

R

real estate, 5, 22, 76, 101, 114
recession, 104
recognition, 104
recommendations, v, 20, 33, 45, 108
recovery, 4, 56, 103, 104, 107, 112, 114
redevelopment, 56
reform, 39
Reform, 25, 43
reforms, 33
regulations, 24, 55, 56, 60, 63, 64, 67, 75, 93
regulatory agencies, 6
regulatory changes, 101
rehabilitation, 35, 107
reliability, 64, 96
relief, 27, 56, 114
requirements, 8, 12, 13, 14, 22, 28, 54, 72, 81, 101
researchers, 27, 28
reserves, 35, 62, 68, 71
resilience, 111
resources, x, 2, 5, 17, 20, 25, 26, 45, 108, 109, 113
response, 29, 101
responsiveness, 30
restrictions, 15, 22, 23
restructuring, 109
retail, 17, 44, 105
revenue, 112
rewards, 21
rights, v
risk, ix, x, 1, 3, 19, 26, 32, 35, 109
rules, 38
rural areas, 92, 100, 105

S

savings, 4, 68, 105, 112, 113
savings account, 68
scope, 43, 64, 100
Secretary of the Treasury, 6, 36, 55, 91
Senate, 6, 16, 17, 18, 23, 24, 25, 31, 33, 40, 41, 43, 45, 61
service organizations, 104
services, v, ix, x, 1, 3, 4, 5, 6, 8, 12, 14, 15, 16, 22, 24, 25, 36, 44, 60, 62, 66, 67, 71, 75, 94, 100, 101, 105, 106, 111, 113
shortage, 4
signals, 27
signs, 55
small businesses, xi, 3, 5, 19, 22, 104, 106, 110
social problems, 104
society, 26
South Dakota, 37
speech, 38
spillovers, 58
stability, 6, 14
staffing, 34
state, xi, 3, 8, 9, 11, 16, 25, 27, 30, 31, 32, 44, 66, 83, 88, 97, 98, 112
states, x, 2, 7, 8, 31, 59
statistics, 12, 60, 111
statutes, 62, 67
stock, 19, 21, 50, 55, 68
structure, 38, 46, 47, 81
subsidy, 21, 24, 29, 30
substitution, 29, 30
substitution effect, 29, 30
success rate, 20
supervision, 24

sustainability, 109
sustainable energy, 112

T

target, 8, 13, 28, 29, 30, 32, 34, 44, 45, 59, 66, 70
tax credits, 19, 20, 27, 50, 54, 58, 59, 62, 63, 65, 68, 77, 78, 81, 87, 88, 91, 95, 106
tax data, 20
tax deduction, 30
tax incentive, 27, 28, 30, 31, 44, 45, 60
taxes, 26, 31, 114
taxpayers, 28, 50
technical assistance, ix, x, 1, 2, 3, 10, 12, 17, 21, 32, 62, 63, 67, 69, 75, 82, 83, 91, 93, 95, 100, 101, 106, 108, 109, 112, 114
technical comments, 91
territory, 8, 9
terrorism, 38
thrifts, 21, 109
time constraints, 93
time frame, 83
time periods, 99
total costs, 29, 30
trade, 29, 30
trade-off, 29, 30
training, 12, 17, 32, 68, 100, 106, 108, 109
transaction costs, 81, 101
transactions, 8, 20, 63, 66, 81, 94
transformation, 111
transparency, 33
Treasury, 6, 18, 23, 24, 31, 33, 36, 38, 42, 46, 47, 51, 56, 91, 107, 114
Treasury Secretary, 33

U

U.S. Bureau of Labor Statistics, 13, 14
U.S. Department of Agriculture, 18
U.S. Department of the Treasury, 38, 42, 46, 47, 50, 103
U.S. economy, 57
underwriting, ix, x, 1, 3
unemployment rate, 13, 14
unions, ix, x, 2, 4, 11, 40, 62, 71, 94, 101, 105, 110
United, vii, xi, xii, 9, 10, 17, 23, 24, 49, 61, 100
United States, vii, xi, xii, 9, 10, 17, 23, 24, 49, 61, 100
urban, 3, 58, 62, 63, 69, 92, 100, 102, 104, 105, 113
urban areas, 63, 92
USA, 7, 25, 113
USDA, 18, 31, 114

V

variations, 27
vehicles, x, 2
venture capital, ix, x, 2, 4, 40, 62, 71, 105
Vice President, 42

W

wages, xi, 3
war, 63, 75, 83, 91, 101, 108
Washington, 7, 37, 38, 40, 41, 43, 45, 46, 47, 100, 101
waste, 111
White House, 33
Wisconsin, 37
workers, 5, 26, 29